WHY WE NEED TO KNOW HOW TO HELP OUR GRIEVING CHILDREN

Each time we cope with the death of someone we flounder. Questions arise: What do we say to the family? How do we tell our children? What should we do to show how much we miss this person? How much should we tell our children? To what extent should children be involved?

The purpose of this book is to help parents through the use of suggestions and examples. Recommendations are carefully and clearly spelled out. There will be no need to sift through philosophical passages hoping to find those special words. Whether the loss is fresh or of several months' duration, there is help.
> —From THE SEASONS OF GRIEF

"This informative and comprehensive book provides parents and helping professionals with practical advice on the important topic of helping children deal with the death of a loved one."
> —Dr. Charles E. Schaefer
> author of HOW TO HELP CHILDREN
> WITH COMMON PROBLEMS

DONNA A. GAFFNEY has a doctorate in psychiatric nursing with a private practice in family therapy. She has taught at several medical and nursing schools and is currently affiliated with the Columbia-Presbyterian School of Medicine. She lives in Summit, New Jersey.

THE SEASONS OF GRIEF

Helping Children Grow Through Loss

by

Dr. Donna A. Gaffney

A PLUME BOOK

NEW AMERICAN LIBRARY

A DIVISION OF PENGUIN BOOKS USA INC., NEW YORK
PUBLISHED IN CANADA BY
PENGUIN BOOKS CANADA LIMITED, MARKHAM, ONTARIO

NAL BOOKS ARE AVAILABLE AT QUANTITY DISCOUNTS WHEN USED TO
PROMOTE PRODUCTS OR SERVICES. FOR INFORMATION PLEASE WRITE
TO PREMIUM MARKETING DIVISION, NEW AMERICAN LIBRARY,
1633 BROADWAY, NEW YORK, NEW YORK 10019.

The Seasons of Grief previously appeared in an NAL BOOKS edition
published by New American Library and published simultaneously
in Canada by The New American Library of Canada Limited
(now Penguin Books Canada Limited).

PLUME TRADEMARK REG. U.S. PAT. OFF. AND FOREIGN COUNTRIES
REG. TRADEMARK—MARCA REGISTRADA
HECHO EN BRATTLEBORO, VT., U.S.A.

SIGNET, SIGNET CLASSIC, MENTOR, ONYX, PLUME, MERIDIAN,
and NAL BOOKS are published *in the United States* by
New American Library, a division of Penguin Books USA Inc.,
1633 Broadway, New York, New York 10019,
in Canada by Penguin Books Canada Limited,
2801 John Street, Markham, Ontario L3R 1B4

Library of Congress Cataloging-in-Publication Data
Gaffney, Donna A.
The seasons of grief.

1. Bereavement—Psychological aspects. 2. Children and death.
3. Parent and child. I. Title.
BF575.G7G34   1988   155.9'37   87-28332
ISBN 0-453-00591-8
ISBN 0-452-26243-7 (pbk.)

First Plume Printing, April, 1989

1   2   3   4   5   6   7   8   9

PRINTED IN THE UNITED STATES OF AMERICA

In memory of
Katie, Lee, and Jimmy

A child's approach to life is refreshing and spontaneous. Children face even those events that adults find intense or traumatic in a matter-of-fact way. Somehow the confusion that initially surrounds their pain gradually resolves, and they emerge, newly resilient.

We can learn a great deal from our children. All we need to do is listen.

ACKNOWLEDGMENTS

I am deeply grateful to all of the families who shared their losses and grieving with me— parents, children, siblings, and friends gave of themselves so that others might grow from their experiences.

I am particularly indebted to Jay Acton, who saw the need for this book and helped me crystallize my ideas in the very beginning. To Alexia Dorszynski, I give my heartfelt thanks for her continued support, sensitivity, and belief in this project.

I give my sincere thanks to my family and friends for all of their encouragement and support. I am grateful to Muriel Evertson for her superb research skills in children's literature. A special note of thanks to Betsy Kuehne for her reading and commenting on early drafts. To Phyllis Paullette MacDougal, my sincere appreciation for always knowing what to say to get me moving again. My love and deepest gratitude to my husband, Jack, for his confidence and encouragement through all of my endeavors. To my children, Ryan, Brendan, and Lauren I give my love and appreciation for teaching me that children are very special indeed.

CONTENTS

INTRODUCTION

The Seasons of Grief

I've written this book for all the mothers, fathers, grandparents, and other adults who have struggled with a child's grief, for all of us who have wanted to make the pain go away and known in our hearts that such a wish would be impossible.

Children have a way of stopping us short in our tracks. They ask us questions that really stump us and tell us about feelings that are truly surprising. The cliché, "out of the mouths of babes" couldn't be more appropriate during the long days of grieving. Whether a child has lost a grandparent, classmate, mother, or father, the pain is real. He can no longer be dismissed with, "They're young, they'll get over it!" The truth is that death is one of life's most significant crises; children will not get over its pain unless we help them deal with it.

The way we deal with loss is through grieving. The emotional work we do to understand and adjust to our loss is called griefwork. It is an intense and unique process with deep feelings, shared experiences, and personal growth. Griefwork takes time and energy. Although our efforts are shared with friends and relatives, griefwork is also a very private experience. The way we grieve depends on a great number of factors: our relationship with the person who has died, our emotional makeup, and our age.

Death is a very difficult experience for all of us to

1

handle. While much has been written about death and griefwork, there is still great confusion about what we should do. Years ago we mourned our dead in the family parlor. Children were expected to take part; it was a family event. In some cases children were even forced to give a kiss to the great aunt in the casket. Then customs changed and grieving was performed publicly, outside the home. Suddenly only adults were supposed to grieve. Children were shuffled off to the sidelines for their own protection. Saying, "It's best that they don't know," we explained very little about what had happened to their dead relative. We went from one extreme to the other. But we are left with the question: What is the best approach for children?

Why We Need to Know How to Help Our Grieving Children

Each time we cope with the death of someone, we flounder. Questions arise: What do we say to the family? How do we tell our children? What should we do to show how much we miss this person? How much should we tell our children? To what extent should children be involved?

It is no accident that most of our concerns focus around children. As parents we want to make the experience of loss as easy as possible. Even as adults, we struggle to write meaningful letters of condolence and offer our help to the grieving family, hoping that in some small way we can make them feel better. When it comes to our children we agonize even more. It takes us longer to find the words and actions that will comfort our young ones. We fear that our saying the wrong things scar our children for life.

Unfortunately, there isn't any one perfect word to make the pain of loss easier. Every situation requires an individual approach. The purpose of this book is to help parents through the use of suggestions and examples. Recommendations are carefully and clearly spelled out. There will be no need to sift through philosophical passages hoping to find those special words. Whether the loss is fresh or of several months' duration, there is help.

Children and the Crisis of Loss

My work with grieving families is based on the concepts of crisis intervention. During a crisis we experience an initial period of disorganization. At that time all of us need support and guidance; children are especially vulnerable during this period. If they are not encouraged to deal with the crisis in their lives their level of functioning will be impaired and they will not return to their precrisis state.

Emerging from a crisis can result in growth. No matter how painful or unpleasant the situation, there is always the opportunity for learning. Children have the most to gain as well as the most to lose. When they face death for the first time, they have no other experiences on which they can rely. Children need their parents and other adults to lead them through such crises. Children given the best possible support will emerge better human beings because of it. In later years they will be able to approach crises as part of life, to be coped with, rather than as something to be paralyzed by.

The Seasons of Grief

My approach with parents is to give support and guidance throughout the crisis of death. I have found that there are five "seasons" of griefwork for children: the first days after the death occurs; the time surrounding funeral or memorial services; the period of reentry following the crisis; the first year; and finally the significant life events of the years ahead. Rather than focusing on particular stages of grief, I suggest that parents use this time frame. We can quickly identify where children are in the process by counting the number of days, weeks, or months since the loss has occurred. The feelings of shock, anger, disbelief, denial, and emptiness occur throughout the seasons of grief. However, the intensity of these feelings fluctuates. Shock, disbelief, and denial prevail during the first few hours following a loss; years later, denial will play a minimal role, while a sense of emptiness may surface on significant holidays and anniversary dates.

Children Are Different

Children's levels of understanding influence how we adults communicate with them. My approach to the seasons of grief is based on the way children think about their world. Children's thinking develops over time just as their bodies develop. This growing ability to understand their environment is called cognitive development. Generally, the older children are, the more they comprehend. We cannot effectively assist children with their coping skills unless we have some knowledge of their stages of cognitive development. My approach to grieving children is presented here in much the same way as I would approach counseling sessions: by communication techniques, concrete suggestions, and by drawing on the experiences of other families.

It is my hope that this book will meet your needs and those of your children through all the seasons of grief.

1

BEGINNINGS

When, How, and What to Tell Your Children When Someone Has Died

Receiving bad news poses a terrible problem for all of us. As parents our first responsibility is to tell our children. But what do we tell them? So often our inclination is to withhold the truth for as long as possible. We hope to spare our children the same pain we ourselves have encountered. In the following pages you will learn when and how to tell your children that someone has died. You will also learn how specific actions can help ease this uncomfortable situation. Children's questions so often leave us searching for the right answers. You'll learn what questions children most commonly ask and how to find the right words for sensitive answers.

Telling Your Children

It is crucial to tell children as soon as possible after a death has occurred. Children will immediately suspect there is something wrong when they observe the body language and silent cues of others. A telephone call in the middle of the night and hushed whispers communicate a message of unknown crisis. Try not to wait until you feel you're "in control" or your tears have dried. Sharing the news right away lets your children know they are included in this family crisis from the very beginning.

"Sandy, come here; we'd like to talk to you. We've just heard from Aunt Emma that your Great Grandma has died. That is why Daddy was crying while he was talking on the telephone."

John's wife was killed in a car accident. His five-year-old daughter was also in the car and witnessed her mother's death. In addition to a child in the intensive care unit John also had a seven-year-old daughter at home. John was called to the hospital knowing that his wife was probably not alive. It was very important for him to tell Kim, the seven-year-old, that her mother would probably die. It took a great deal of courage for him to say the following words:

"There has been a car accident. It looks like Mom is hurt very badly but Cindy will be okay. I need to go to the hospital right now. Grandma will be here with you. I will be back as soon as I can. I love you."

John's decision probably left his daughter wondering what was going on at the hospital. However, if he had not told her the situation Kim would have felt betrayed by him. As it was, he was honest and gave no false hopes. Kim was distressed that her father had to leave, but there are no ideal solutions.

Tell Your Children Personally

It is usually best to tell children personally that someone has died. Unless circumstances prevent it, parents are the best people to give the news. The reason for this is that after you have told your child what has happened as clearly and simply as possible you can then reach out to each other with a hug or some other sign of affection. This initial exchange between parents and children forms the foundation for working through the grieving process in the coming weeks and months.

Sometimes it is difficult to tell children early because the news of a death has come by telephone, quite suddenly, necessitating a trip to the hospital. For those times when a parent or parents have to leave their families, it is best for children to be with people who are caring and aware of the situation. For children as well as adults "not knowing" is more difficult to handle than the truth. We don't know whether to remain hopeful or to begin to grieve the loss. Because their main worry will be for their parents, children find this waiting period filled with fantasies and fears. As soon as possible you should reunite with your children to confirm what has happened.

Beth learned of her father's death by telephone one morning. She was twelve years old, and her father had been sick for several weeks. She was with a trusted family friend while her mother was with her father at the hospital. When the telephone rang, Beth said later, "I knew something was wrong, I knew my father was dead." Beth took the telephone and her mother could only say to her, "Your daddy has gone to heaven." Beth was stunned; she wanted to cry but felt she couldn't because her mother was not with her. She was comforted by the presence of an understanding adult, but at the same time wanted to be "strong" for this friend so her mother would get a "good report." Only later was Beth finally able to resolve the anger she felt toward her mother for not being with her; she had carried this feeling for over twenty-five years.

A Comfortable, Secure Setting

Do not hurry when you tell your children tragic news. Find a quiet and comfortable spot. Children will feel better if they are in familiar surroundings—in a playroom, on a soft couch, or in a favorite corner. Although Diane, a thirty-year-old woman, could not recall the circumstances of her grandfather's death or funeral, she did vividly remember her father sitting and talking with her about her feelings at the little play table in her room. Diane was only five and a half years old at the time.

Reach Out to Your Children

A gentle hug, a kiss on the forehead, or even a tearful embrace will give more support and comfort to children than words. Holding your children's hands or putting your arm around their shoulders as you talk to them will communicate a warmth and caring that they will remember long after the painful words.

Simple, Honest Explanations

Finding the right words to tell children about the death of someone close to them is not an easy task. Often we use words that we think are less frightening. As a result children may be confused and unsure about the information they are hearing.

Use Words That Are Clear and Concrete

Don't equate death with the words "sleep," "a trip to heaven," or "gone away." Because younger children interpret information in a very concrete way these words may prove alarming and add to concerns for their own survival. Ten-year-old Jerry had been told from the time he was a small boy that when people die they go to heaven where there are dozens of flavors of ice cream. When Jerry's great-aunt died he attended the funeral. He repeatedly asked his mother why people were crying. "Why aren't they happy? I wish it were me and I could eat as much ice cream as I wanted!" In an attempt to make heaven and death seem a positive experience to her small boy, Jerry's mother had reinforced an unrealistic perception. It will take a great deal of work to undo Jerry's misconceptions of death.

Consider Your Child's Age When Choosing Your Words

Language should be geared to children's level of understanding. The best indicator of this level is their age and grade in school.

Preschoolers

Explain death to very young children by comparing it to the parts of life they already know. When people die they no longer breathe or eat, and they cannot see their family or friends anymore. A child under the age of five will not be able to understand details of an illness or body organs. Preschoolers generally have some sense that certain diseases are "bad" but they don't know why.

If a grandparent dies as a result of a long illness, describe the situation from the information the child already has. When Lauren's babysitter of five years died at the age of forty-two from cancer, her mother explained:

> "Remember how I told you that Sandy was very sick? Well, her body just could not fight against this sickness anymore, and she died. We won't be able to see her anymore; she won't babysit for you or your brothers."

At five years of age Lauren would not have a knowledge of cancer, chemotherapy, or the effects of the disease.

Keep repeating explanations in clear, simple words. Very young children will seem to be denying what has been told to them. Because of their stage of development you may not be able to convince your children of the circumstances of death. Patience is especially important with the preschooler. As your children grow they will eventually understand the meaning of what has happened, and then they will be ready to ask more questions.

School-Age Children

School-age children have a curiosity about death and the rituals that surround it in our society. They no longer view death as something magical or reversible. Questions raised by six- to eleven-year-old children can encompass a vast array of information. Simply telling children of this age that someone has died will not be adequate. They are very interested in the functioning of the human body. Samantha's great-grandmother died unexpectedly of a heart attack. Samantha's mother tried to explain to her daughter exactly what happened but didn't want to get too technical, so she settled for "her heart stopped because it was old and tired." Samantha began to draw her own conclusions. At ten years old she was fairly certain that she didn't have to worry about her own heart stopping but was wondering how her great-grandmother could be fine one day and dead the next.

Use general explanations that are specific but not complex or advanced. For school-age children technical discussions will be far too sophisticated, so give an explanation in general terms.

> "Great-Grandma's heart was not as healthy as yours or mine. When people get very old their hearts change. Sometimes the blood vessels bringing blood to the heart become narrow and stiff. When this happens the right amounts of food and oxygen do not get to the heart to keep it strong."

You do not have to provide specific pathology, unless the child is interested and capable of understanding.

Teenagers

A different approach is needed when telling a teenager or preadolescent of someone's death. Not only are they able to understand more complex physiologic explanations but they are also aware of the psychological and spiritual or religious aspects of death. Give thoughtful, complete explanations.

Include teenagers in planning for the funeral and beyond but do not use them for adultlike support. It is tempting to use adolescents as a support since they are adultlike in so many ways. However, relying on teenagers for advice, guidance, or even decision making can have a disastrous impact on their grieving processes. Even though teenagers have a greater intellectual understanding of loss, the grieving experience presents a number of emotional hurdles. How many times have we heard a well-meaning relative say to a young man who has just lost his father, "Well, you will have to be the man of the family now. Your mother will really need you"? The message to the adolescent is "Grow up fast— you have new and added responsibilities." While it is certain that there will be added dimensions to his role, grieving must come first.

Circumstances of Death

While we never truly feel prepared for the loss of someone close to us, our emotional reactions often depend on the circumstances of that person's death. We seem to have an easier adjustment when we lose someone who has lived a long, productive life. A peaceful death is easier for us to accept than a death filled with violence. We may have an especially difficult time when young persons die suddenly from an accident; we are shocked that people so young will not finish out their lives. It is difficult to see another's pain, yet when someone is ill we have a chance to prepare for death by grieving ahead of time. Children too are susceptible to these different circumstances. They need a chance to understand the situation and work it through. I will explore some of these circumstances here and in Chapter 5.

Anticipating Death After a Long Illness

Do not exclude children from visits to the dying.

Michael and Ricky understood that their babysitter, their Aunt Sal, had cancer and they feared that she could die from the disease. At first Sal did not want the children to know that she had cancer but the side effects of potent drugs and radiation were difficult to hide. The boys had many questions about her course of treatment: How long would it take for the medicine to make her better? When would her hair grow back? And when would she be able to take care of them again? Susan, the boys' mother, decided to bring the children to the hospital to see their babysitter for what she believed might be the last time. Each child made his own choice about visiting.

Give factual information about the illness. The two school-age boys were very upset when told of their aunt's death a few days later. They asked questions that centered around their knowledge of her illness. Ricky said, "Aunt Sal just didn't seem the same to me." Seeing Sal in the hospital prior to her death helped the boys to realize the extent of her illness. Their experience in the hospital made the death seem more real to them, and they could begin to work through their feelings of grief. We adults often think that seeing a person very ill and in the hospital will frighten children and lead to painful, unpleasant memories. However, allowing children to either confirm or deny thoughts of how a very ill person looks is useful and will ultimately facilitate the griefwork they must do. By contrast, when children rely on their fantasies for information, rather than reality, those imagined memories linger on. But the decision must be the child's; parents and other concerned adults must remember not to force a child to visit a sick relative or friend.

Don't give false hope to children. Assuring your children that all will be well does little to provide a sense of security. Honesty counts heavily at these times. Children need to be prepared for the future.

"Aunt Sal has been very sick with cancer for a long time, and her body is worn out from fighting the disease. The medicine doesn't kill the cancer cells anymore, and she has become very weak. She probably won't live much longer. This will be sad for all of us. Whenever you want to talk about Aunt Sal, it's okay because it's better if we share our feelings with each other."

When Death Comes Suddenly

The sudden loss of someone we love renders us helpless. Totally unprepared for what has happened, we fight reality as long as possible. Children do not understand these situations any better than adults. Your role as a parent will include continual reinforcement of the reality of what has happened, and acknowledgment of the shock and disbelief your child experiences.

Mary Beth was eleven years old when she came home from school to find her home filled with relatives and the curtains drawn. She knew from the drawn curtains, an old English custom of respect for the dead, that her mother had died. She recalls being in a state of shock, not being able to "put one foot in front of the other." A policeman had to help her cross the street. The rest of the day was a blur. Her memory of that painful day causes tearfulness every time she hears the song "Oh What A Beautiful Morning," which was playing on the radio as she entered her home and learned her mother died. Mary Beth was whisked off to the home of another relative. She did not have time to talk about her feelings or even attend the funeral. Even though it took

Mary Beth years to recover from her sudden loss she was able to channel her "lesson" into productive parenting for her own children. She knew that she could never let her own children experience what she had; she has shared their losses with them.

Special Circumstances: Death in the Classroom, the Community, the Nation

The death of a child or teacher in the school or the community can have a ripple effect on many children. At first it seems that only children in the immediate family and classmates are touched by the loss. But such an event can have multiple layers, like fragile onion skin, with its many layers adhering to each other.

Steven was in second grade when he was diagnosed with acute leukemia. His illness followed a stormy course; he missed many days at school, and after eleven months of unsuccessful treatment he died. The loss was felt by his second-grade classmates. But there were others who also felt Steven's death: the schoolmates of Steven's older sixth-grade brother and the children in his older sister's fourth-grade class.

Parents, teachers, and other concerned adults can help children understand what has happened in the context of their classroom. No matter how distant a child might be to the death, he can learn new growth-promoting skills. Teachers and parents can help by encouraging children to talk to each other. For very young children discussions should be brief and structured. Familiar surroundings and familiar people will help. Even kindergartners and first graders will feel some comfort hearing the questions and feelings of their peers. Teachers can also use picture drawing and story telling to encourage further class discussion. For older children classroom discussions can be longer and more detailed. Often children will want to hear facts and ask questions about the event.

Children who have witnessed the death of a classmate or teacher will need more support. Some children may have trouble returning to the place where the death occurred; others may reenact the death in dramatic play. Either reaction is normal and should not be interpreted as bizarre or uncaring. If you see your children behaving in any of these ways, use the situation as an opportunity to talk about the loss and about their feelings.

> "I noticed you pretending to fall off the swing in our backyard. I'm wondering if that reminds you of Jamie's accident. It must be hard to go back to the playground at school and see the place where Jamie died. If it were me I think I'd feel sad. What about you?"

Sometimes we don't feel comfortable when our children talk about death in school. Our first instinct is to be there, to soften the words and give a hug so it won't hurt as much. But children need to be with their peers to work out these potentially traumatic events. Your role is to encourage your child to talk about these class discussions at home.

> "I'm wondering if your class talked about Jamie today in school. What did you think about it? Is there anything that you heard that puzzles you? Or maybe even is a bit scary?"

Through these opportunities you can reinforce the facts and clarify misconceptions. At the same time you let the children know that it is all right to share their thoughts and feelings with peers, an activity that prepares them for coping with other crises in their lives. If you have any concerns about your children's behavior, don't hesitate to share this with their teachers. Together you can work out a plan to help your children cope with death both in the classroom and at home.

National tragedies have a way of affecting our lives in very profound ways. The death of someone we "knew" as a hero or of an important member of our society has a strong psychological impact. In 1963 the nation mourned the loss of a president. Parents who were children at that time vividly remember hearing the news; they remember where they were and what they were doing. Twenty-three years later seven astronauts were killed in the tragic accident of the *Challenger* explosion. We were expecting a joyous occasion and instead experienced a tragedy. Our children were very involved because of the educational nature of the shuttle launch. Every child who watched was a witness to seven deaths. The children observed not only the accident but the emotional reactions of family and friends.

The day after the space shuttle *Challenger* exploded, one kindergarten class was talking about the accident. It was obvious that the children knew the astronauts had died. They were filled with questions, but more than that, they had solutions. There was a magical quality surrounding their explanations: a "fire-copter" could put out the fire or the astronauts could parachute to safety. After a brief discussion the teacher asked the children to draw pictures and then asked them what they would like to do with them. The class decided that they would like to send their artwork to the school of the schoolteacher, Christa McAuliffe.

These children were young but certainly aware that seven human beings had died. Because of their developmental stage these five- and six-year-olds did not completely understand the nature of the tragedy, but they could still grieve and share their feelings.

There is a difference between mourning the loss of someone we know well and someone who is distant from us. There is an intensity of emotion in the beginning for both situations. However, when the loss is more distant our griefwork can be accomplished in a shorter period of time. We experience a pervasive sadness but there are not major changes in our lives. We share our feelings with other people, mourn, and then go on. When our children express feelings of grief at such events, we need to encourage them to share their thoughts, not minimize their reaction because the death wasn't "in the family."

Denial and Anger

Children as well as adults experience a deep sense of shock and disbelief during the first hours following a loss. Your task is to recognize your child's feelings while you continue to focus on reality.

Terry was a strong, agile eleven-year-old Boy Scout. His accidental death on a camping trip tore into the hearts of his playmates and their families. Upon hearing the sad news from his parents, Terry's friend Brent shouted angrily, "It's not true, it didn't happen. I just don't believe it!" He walked away in a huff, leaving his bewildered parents speechless. At such a point it is essential that you acknowledge your child's sense of disbelief and then firmly reinforce reality.

"I know this is hard for you to believe. I can't even believe it myself, but it is true— Terry died today and we are all very sad."

Days or weeks may go by before your child begins to accept the reality of what has happened. Sometimes the sense of disbelief may come and go. Remember that this is all a part of early griefwork and fills a need for your child. Children tend to give up denial when they are ready to move on to sharing their grieving.

Sensitive Answers to Difficult Questions

Can it happen to me? Will you die, too?

This is a question that parents will have to address. Grieving children often fear that they will succumb to the same set of circumstances as the person who has died. It is best for parents to initiate the discussion by bringing up the possibility that those fears do exist. Once parents admit that death scares everyone, children will not feel so alone.

"Sometimes when we hear that a person has died we think it might happen to us or someone we love."

Assure children of the differences between a person's cause of death and the child's own health status. Of course, when someone quite a bit older dies it makes our job easier, as in this case. When a younger person dies it is more difficult for all of us to handle, so our reassurances will be harder to give. During these times we must comfort children that such occurrences are rare and that most of us will live long, healthy lives.

"Grandma's heart was not young and strong like yours. Your heart is working just as it should and it will be strong and healthy for a long, long time."

Why didn't the doctors and medicines make my aunt better? Why did she have to die?

"Sometimes the best medicines and the best doctors do all they can to make people better but their bodies are too sick and they die. When that happens we have many questions that we want answered and we all feel confused."

Who will take care of me, get me ready for school, and make my lunch?

"I know we can't imagine how we will get by without Mom right now. The important thing to remember is that we are all together and will help each other. We will take one step at a time, very slowly, and it will all work out. It just takes time."

As parents we often feel that we must give our children answers to all their questions. In most cases children do not really want answers but rather a chance to verbalize their feelings. Sharing our own thoughts gives our children a chance to know us better. For the most part, children want the reassurance of knowing that others feel the same way they do.

Asking for Help

Sometimes you will feel that you cannot take on the entire responsibility for talking with your child. The situation is too painful for both of you. You do not have to do it alone. While is no substitute for a parent's words of love and support for children, if you truly cannot talk to your child at this difficult time, get someone to help you. Your mate, a trusted friend, another family member—anyone who makes you feel comfortable. They will not do the work for you, but they can hold your hand and help you through the tough parts as you help your child.

There is so much to know and do in these first hours of your crisis. How can you possibly remember it all? Take each step as it comes. If the words don't come out right the first time, try again and again if necessary. Through your openness your children will know that it is okay for them to be the same way. The days ahead will not be easy, but they can be a time for sharing your grief with those around you.

2

SHARING YOUR GRIEF

Including Your Children in Memorial Services

As parents we are faced with the difficult task of deciding how to include our children in funeral and memorial services. Sometimes the question is not how to involve children but whether they should be present at all. Fifty years ago families mourned their dead in the parlor. Home funerals were as commonplace as home births. Often small children were forced to kiss or touch the dead person. I know many fifty- and sixty-year-old people who remember such events with great anxiety. When those traumatized children grew up they vowed to spare their own youngsters the same pain. The less their children knew about funerals, wakes, and burials, they reasoned, the better off they would be. But when they are thus "protected," children are aware of being excluded and carry the empty space and the "not knowing" with them for the rest of their lives.

How much do you urge your children to participate without forcing? And how much do you keep from them without sheltering? There has to be a middle ground. The wisest advice I can give is to take cues from your children themselves. They cannot make all decisions by themselves, but with your guidance, they will have a good sense of what they want to do. On the following pages you will learn how to answer frequently asked questions and deal with your children's reactions to formal mourning rites.

Making the Decision:
Should We Include the Children?

Children need to focus on formal mourning events in a specific and positive way. This is not a time for children to see what dead people look like or to satisfy their curiosity. When a parent or teacher approaches a child about going to a funeral, wake, or memorial service, the reason for the child's attendance should not be that "it is time he went to a funeral" but that there is a special meaning in the loss of the person to that child. Making the decision for children to participate is not easy. Children are individuals with different needs under different circumstances, and it would be a mistake to make uniform suggestions on this sensitive topic. There are, however, some important general guidelines to consider as you make your decisions.

If a member of the immediate family has died, every effort should be made to include children from at least the age of three years. While this may seem a bit early, even very young children will benefit from the experience. Toddlers and preschoolers will not understand the circumstances but they will be able to take in the event on their own level.

It is important to remember that the level of participation in services should be related to a child's age. While two- or three-year-olds will not understand or acknowledge that a family member is dead from looking at the body, they will remember the brief moments their parents carried them into the funeral home. As children take in the visual experience parents can use gentle words to explain that they will no longer be able to talk or play with that special person who has died. Although an older child will be able to endure longer periods of involvement, remember that breaks and rest times outside of the funeral home or church may be needed.

Preparation Is the Key

When there is a death in the immediate family the most useful information to convey to your child is the idea that the days of formal mourning will be very, very busy. There will be lots of activity, with many people surrounding the family. Recall the times that you have gone to a funeral or a wake or visited a family after the death of a loved one; the day or even the few hours spent in services are intense and emotionally and physically exhausting. Multiply those feelings by three or four days and you have the experience of a child who has lost a member of the immediate family.

Children who will be attending the services of a relative, friend, or community member will also have to understand the feeling of busy-ness when attending these formal mourning rites. Explain that many people will come to honor the life of the person who has died and give words of comfort to close family and friends.

What Happens at a Formal Service?

Funerals, Wakes, and Memorial Services

Tell your children that formal or public expressions of grief can occur in several ways. Families decide what they would like to do based on their religious and ethnic backgrounds. Local customs also help a family decide how they will share their grief with the community. Your explanation should begin with those customs most familiar to you and likely to be observed by your own family. Some brief explanations you might use are:

"A wake is a period of time when people come to visit the family of the person who has died. This is called 'paying your respects' to the dead. Wakes are usually held in a funeral home or in the family's home. The casket holding the dead person is in the room. It might be open or closed, depending on the family's wishes. There are special times for people to visit. The wake may last one, two, or three days. Visitors look at the casket, and talk to the family and other visitors. It is a time when everyone shares their feelings of grief with each other and the family."

When describing a funeral you might say:

"Funerals are services that take place before someone is buried. Funerals can be held in a funeral home or in a church. Relatives and people who knew the dead person come to the service. There may be prayers, readings, eulogies (short speeches telling about the person who has died), and music. In some religions the funeral takes place at a mass, or special church service. After the funeral, family members follow the hearse to the cemetery. At the gravesite more prayers may be said by the minister, rabbi, or priest."

It is important to talk about the difference between a funeral and a memorial service:

"A memorial service can take place after the person has been buried or cremated or, in some cases, when the body of the dead person has not been found. Memorial services can take place in churches, temples, or any other place where large numbers of people can gather—schools, government buildings, or even parks. The memorial service has many of the same things that a funeral has: prayers, readings, eulogies, and sometimes music. The difference between the two is that after a memorial service there is no burial."

The best approach to preparing children for any kind of formal service is to explain to them *ahead of time* what they can expect. This explanation should include the time frame for events and what people will be there, as well as the visual experience that they will be exposed to. Very young children will want to take in every aspect of the environment. Often, what is overlooked or taken for granted by adults may be the focus of immense curiosity by children. Preparing them includes describing the physical appearance, smells, and feelings of the setting. The description should be factual; it need not be morbid or gloomy. Use words or analogies that are familiar to your children.

Some important aspects to include are:

- The physical layout of the room:
    How big is it?
    How are the chairs placed?
    Where are the doorways?
    Is there a casket in the room?
    Where is the casket located?

- The appearance of the room:
    What is the color of the room?
    Are there flowers?
    How many flowers are there and where are they?

- The casket's appearance:
    How long is it? (Compare it to a table or other piece of furniture.
    What is the color or texture of the wood?
    Is the casket open?
    What does the inside look like? (Describe the pillow, lining, etc.)

Once you have described these less frightening aspects you can then proceed to the more upsetting parts of the experience.

We all fantasize about seeing a dead person. It is perhaps the most chilling of human experiences. Children are filled with questions and curiosity. They are repelled and attracted at the same time. Because this part of the mourning process is so frightening it is important to prepare children for seeing a dead person, especially when it will be for the first time. Although we know that we need to describe the physical appearance of a nonliving body to children accurately, we hesitate because it is difficult to talk about the characteristics of a dead body, or because we may not want to upset our children any more than necessary. But giving factual information will not add to a child's anxiety, while a lack of information may lead to fantasies that feed a child's fears.

Try to avoid using the analogy of sleep or sleeplike appearance at any time. Children, especially younger children, may equate sleep with death. It is too easy to say "Aunt Mary will look just like she is sleeping." The truth is that Aunt Mary looks nothing like that at all. Instead use clear, unambiguous words that will help children visualize what they can expect:

"Aunt Mary's body will be lying down in the casket. Only the top half of the casket will be open, so we won't be able to see her feet or legs. There will be a pillow underneath her head. The people at the funeral home will try to make Aunt Mary's hair and face look like they did when she was alive but it will not be the same. Her eyes will be shut. Her hands will probably be folded. You can touch her hands if you want. The skin will feel cool and firm. It will not feel like Aunt Mary when she was alive. I will be there next to you. You won't be alone."

Begin by describing the position of the body, hair, facial appearance, clothing, and the hands. If there are any objects in the casket with the body, mention this as well. Children will often ask if jewelry or other items will be buried with the body. If you know the answer tell your child. If not, mention the fact that families sometimes feel strongly that certain favorite things should be buried with the body. Other times family members want to keep such items for the people who are still living, as a reminder of the person who has died.

Children need to know what others will be doing so they are not confused or frightened. When children witness formal mourning, they may not understand conversations they hear or their tone; talk among relatives sometimes seems to have a lighter quality, due to the fact that many of the people present may not have seen each other for a long time. Children may expect that everyone will be very sad and crying. While this is true for part of the time there may be periods when there is smiling and maybe even some laughter. Children need to be told that this doesn't mean that people do not care or are not interested.

Explaining Funeral Customs and Rituals to Your Child

Encountering services that are unfamiliar can be confusing to parents and children alike. Behavior of family members and clergy may seem strange at first. Simple explanations will help children appreciate these differences and feel comfortable enough to ask more questions. The following are brief descriptions of the ways various religious and ethnic groups mourn the dead.

- Many religious groups believe that people go on to another life after they have died. Roman Catholics, in particular, believe that the funeral mass is a celebration of both the person's life on earth and his going to heaven to be with God. Most Catholics talk about the "happiness" of the person who has died now that he will be with God. If a person is dying it is very important for the priest to be present to give "last rites," in which the priest helps the person ask for forgiveness from God for wrongdoings during life. Catholic funerals are usually held in a church, and burials take place in a Catholic cemetery. It would be unusual for a casket to be open during the mass, although it may be open during the wake. Catholics generally do not approve of cremation, although it is becoming more accepted today.

- When a Fundamentalist dies the preacher talks to the congregation about the good deeds this person has done while alive. Fundamentalists believe that a person is judged at the moment of death by God. A person who has been good will go to heaven; a person who has sinned against God may not receive "eternal salvation." Funerals and burials are generally very emotional, with the preacher talking about good and evil and the eternal happiness the person has earned. There may be readings or quotations from the Bible and talk of the beauty of heaven.

- More mainstream Protestant religions also believe that death is very important. Their explanation of how a person gets to heaven may not be as explicitly defined as the Catholic or Fundamentalist religions. Funeral customs vary among the different denominations, individual families, and local customs of observance. Services can take place in a church or in the funeral home.

- Judaism stresses the importance of life, and its rituals offer great comfort to the family of the person who has died. Traditional practices provide a system of planned support for family members throughout the time of grief. In the Jewish religion, it is customary to bury the dead as soon as possible. Following the funeral there is a special meal prepared called the "meal of consolation" for the immediate family. For the next week the family remains at home receiving relatives and friends; since the family is not allowed to prepare meals, visitors bring food. This period of seven days is called "Shivah." The family of the person who has died sits on furniture that is lower than usual and may wear torn garments or small pieces of cloth that have been torn. These activities symbolize the mourning period of the family. These first seven days are not a time of socializing or entertainment but of grieving. Sometimes the men will not shave or the women wear makeup, and mirrors are covered in the home. Again, these are signs of the grieving time for families.

- Religions of the Far East have customs very different from those of the Western world. Some religions teach that the spirit of the person who has died will find a home in a new body; this is called "reincarnation." After a person dies the body is draped in clean white clothes or cloth. Visitors come to pay their respects to the family, but only the family attends the funeral. The body is then cremated. The family begins a period of praying that lasts for the next ten days. Their belief is that this helps the soul find a new body. After those days have passed, the family share food and gifts from friends and relatives to celebrate the new home of the soul. In some Eastern religions dying people are bathed in rivers to cleanse their bodies in preparation for death. In other religions, lanterns are floated on the rivers or canals during the funeral ceremony.

   Funeral customs and rituals may also vary with a family's cultural or ethnic background. The behavior of the family and mourners may vary surprisingly from one culture to the next.

- In traditional Irish families funerals are very important social events; the wake may be the most significant family gathering of the year. There is often much celebrating, joking, and laughter, along with remembering of the dead. A family may even take pictures of all the aunts, uncles, and cousins at the wake.

- In families of Hispanic origin, particularly Puerto Ricans, people are very expressive of their feelings when a person has died. Roman Catholic masses and other rituals involving prayer are used to help mourn the loss. Relatives gather at the funeral and openly express their emotions, sometimes in dramatic ways. To a non-Hispanic, the crying, wailing, and other outpourings of grief may appear exaggerated or hysterical. However, their effusiveness doesn't mean that Hispanics have difficulty coping with the death; rather, it is a cultural custom for families to be so open.

- Families of Mediterranean descent, such as Italians and Greeks, are also very open in the sharing of their grief. One young woman recalled attending her first Italian funeral. She was not prepared for the almost hysterical grieving at the side of the casket. Each family member openly cried, sobbed, and lamented. There was much discussion of the death of the person, and each time a mourner returned to the casket the feelings were openly expressed again.

- The church, especially the Baptist church, is a very meaningful part of the lives of many black American families. The wake is an important time for friends and relatives to mourn the loss of the dead. There is much crying and other open expression of grief. The preacher and other church officials play prominent roles in the formal grieving services. Funeral services are filled with songs and music. A good example is the typical New Orleans funeral, which includes a procession through the streets accompanied by musicians playing brass instruments.

It is quite appropriate for children to visit friends or relatives to offer condolences, no matter what their religion or ethnic background. Children will feel especially helpful if they can bring some food or a small gift for the family. If time permits they may even want to make the food or wrap it themselves. Most children are curious about the traditions observed by other families. Parents can contact a friend or acquaintance of the same religion or ethnic background as the person who has died and ask about customary practices of mourning. If parents do not have anyone to ask, a telephone call to the community church, temple, or cultural organization will be helpful.

Participation in Formal Services

When children are given a role in formal grieving services they can begin to work through their feelings of loss or grief. Children need to feel useful in almost everything they do. Attending a funeral or memorial service honoring the life of someone who has died is certainly no different. By having some kind of role your child will feel a sense of accomplishment and satisfaction about having been able to help. As parents we may think that participation might be too much for our children—too trying or too difficult. But this is not the case at all. The experience of participation is something that children will be able to recollect in the years ahead, not with a feeling of anguish or trauma but often with warm feelings of remembrance for the person they miss.

Experiencing a loss thrusts us into a dizzying spiral of confusion. We are out of control. We can't change the course of events. Try as we might to make sense of the ordeal, we can't. By contributing in a small way we begin to feel in control. Such contributions, no matter how insignificant they seem in the greater scheme, help us begin to resolve that terrifying sense of helplessness. Children experiencing the mysterious customs of mourning will benefit from taking part in services, although their participation depends on their age and their relationship with the person who has died.

What Your Child Can Do

There are a number of things you and your child can do to feel a part of the formal grieving services. Your child's relationship to the person who has died will help you decide what is appropriate and comfortable.

It is not always a good idea to stress a child's formal participation in services when a parent has died—being close to the surviving parent or grandparents during formal mourning services is more important. Children feel the loss and separation of a parent most acutely. It is better for them to be with a person who can give love and a sense of security during the services. Being with an adult who answers questions, dries tears, and provides comfort will help children feel a part of the services even if they do not have a formal role. There is plenty of time for children to take part in memorial activities for their parent after the first two weeks.

When children lose a brother or sister, their formal participation can be accomplished in a number of ways. The roles do not have to be extensive or require a great deal of concentration. This is a time for a small but meaningful contribution to the funeral or memorial services by the surviving siblings. When their brother died, Keith and Brett were confused by all the activities surrounding the funeral services. A close family friend helped the boys' parents plan a funeral service that would have meaning and offer roles for both brothers and for their dead son's friends. The following program was from the "celebration" of Joey's life.

Celebrating the Life of
Joseph Alan White

Prelude .... Wesley Brighton
Tolling of the Church Bells ..... Keith and
Brett White
Opening Words and Invocation .. Rev. A. Traxton
Solo of the Lord's Prayer .... Nina Kravatts
Readings from the Old Testament
Readings from poetry and prose
Readings from the New Testament Pastor J. Anders
Five Friends .... Christopher
Brenda
Mark
Karl
Michael
Color Guard .... Troop #39, Boy
Scouts of America
Donald Thomas,
Scoutmaster
Prayer
Commendation
A Memorial Moment
Postlude and Recessional .... The Hallelujah
Chorus

This was a most touching service for everyone who attended. Adults are not used to children participating in
such a prominent way. At first some parents were shocked
that their children would play a part in the services.
But the children wanted to participate and even wrote
their own "letters," which were read in front of the
congregation of mourners. Joey's brothers, who were
younger than these friends who would read from the
pulpit, rang the church bells at the beginning of the

service—a meaningful yet uncomplicated task. After they were finished they joined their parents, staying close to them for the rest of the service.

Joey's friends had roles that required thought and bravery, as they read their letters to the members of the congregation. Christopher and Mark, both age eleven, wanted to share their letters with the readers of this book.

To Joey from Chris

Joey White was a tall, good-looking boy. He had brownish hair with eyebrows that matched equally. He had quite a strapping body.

Joey was very good in school, he got mostly A's, with a couple of B's stuck in there too. He was very good in math. After almost every test he'd ask me what I got. He would usually have a higher grade than I would.

In sports he played football, basketball, and he wrestled and he swam. He had lots of stamina and was quite a kid!

Joey and I did lots of things together because we were very close friends. We built a tree house. We went downtown together to buy either books, candy, or stereo cassettes. We would climb trees and watch TV. We would ride bikes or go on hikes. Joey was quite an active boy, and I loved him!

To Joey from Mark

We are here today to give our last respects to Joey White. I would like to say a few things about him. Joey was one of my closest friends. We would play a lot together. We had so much fun together. We played football, Dungeons and Dragons, and guns together. Many of Joey's friends are here today also to say good-bye. I hope that you will pray for him. Thank you.

The words of children do not have to be formal or eloquent eulogies. These two letters simply tell of the relationships the writers had with their friend.

Don't try to help your children write letters or condolence notes. Let them think about what they want to say and struggle with the words a bit. Have them read their work to you when they are finished, if they wish. Such rehearsing has two benefits: Your child will become familiar with the words and will also begin to grieve the loss of the special relationship with the friend.

Other Ways to Participate

Friends, brothers, and sisters can participate in funeral or memorial services in a number of different ways. For example, in Catholic or Episcopal masses there may be roles of altar server, scripture reader, or presenter of gifts. One family in particular wanted to personalize the mass for their dead son, an avid football player who died in an accident. During the part of the mass when gifts were brought to the altar to symbolize the offering of part of oneself to God, the family brought up his football uniform. His uniform and football equipment were then donated to a sports program in the community.

Occasionally families decide to use brothers and friends as pallbearers at funerals. This is a memorable experience for both observer and participant. Who among us can forget young Robert Kennedy, Jr., struggling under the weight of his father's casket? Again, remember to ask your child if this is something that he would like to do. When Joey White was buried, the older of his brothers, Brett, was a pallbearer. Brett looks back on the experience with pride. "I felt good that I could do something for my brother."

Some Guidelines

Participation in memorial or funeral services is an individual decision. Children need to be asked if they would like to participate and then be encouraged to decide for themselves what they will say or write. If there is an activity they are being asked to perform, describe fully the role to your children so they can make an educated decision. Telling your children that their role will take only a "few minutes" or will be "so simple" may lead to anxiety if their part turns out to be anything more. Be honest. Find out the scope of the role and prepare your children for the experience.

Some children want very much to be a part of formal mourning services; others do not— the decision must be left to them. If you as the parent have a great desire to have your children participate, be as objective as you can when presenting the request. You may even consider asking in such a way that your children think it is their own idea. Forcing or pushing them to do something they are not willing to do will only lead to resentment toward you. The grieving experience is painful enough.

Finding the Right Words

One of the most difficult and uncomfortable experiences for all of us is greeting a friend or relative who has experienced a death in the family. We struggle with the challenge of finding the right words. Somehow "I'm sorry" seems a weak and meaningless expression for the intensity of feelings we have for the person who has died. And receiving the words of others is equally uncomfortable for the grieving family. I've heard parents murmur "Thank you" time after time, expressions of kindness frozen on their faces for hours, as visitors expressed feelings of sadness.

Accepting Condolences

What should we say when people offer words of sympathy to us? Children may be especially perplexed about this. As parents and other concerned adults we often don't think about "the right words"; we've had enough experience to know what to do. But it *is* hard to find the right words. You may find yourself nodding or smiling weakly when someone extends condolences. It is especially important for us to prepare children in similar situations. At wakes, funerals, or memorial services, great numbers of people approach children with words of concern. These moments can overwhelm even the most mature adult. Children need to know what to say. Some very useful responses for children are: "Thank you very much," "It makes me feel good that you care," or even "I'm glad you could come today." It is far easier for children to remember one of these phrases rather than trying to say something that is individualized for each visitor. It is also helpful to explain to children the reason for thanking people who have come to visit the family of the deceased.

"It is very hard for people to come and pay respects after a person has died. Truthfully, people find this quite difficult and may even try to avoid these times. So when someone comes to visit us, it is because they care so very much about us. We need to thank our friends and family for sharing our sadness."

There are times when children and other survivors in the family feel as though they are providing comfort and support to visitors at a funeral or wake. While this is not at all unusual, children need to be told that they may have this experience.

Debbie and Tom had lost their eleven-year-old son in a tragic boating accident. They decided that a wake would be important for their son's friends and the family. There were two daughters to consider, and they too would be a part of the mourning services. Some of their neighbors came and started to cry. The girls saw their mother hug them and tell them everything would be all right. Abbie and Leslie were quite surprised to see their parents consoling and comforting other people who came to see their dead brother. They asked each other, "Shouldn't this be the other way around?"

Children witnessing this phenomenon may feel a sense of unfairness and possibly even anger. Tell your children that immediate family members have had several hours or even days together to share their feelings of grief. Of course, the feelings are not yet resolved but the family is together and have supported each other through the first difficult hours. Visitors meeting with the family for the first time after a death are confronted with shock and disbelief. They are also confronted with the intense feelings and emotions of the survivors. And so it seems as though visitors are more upset than family members and are comforted by the very people who have suffered the loss. There is a simple way to explain this experience to children:

"I know it seems like you and I are helping your aunt to feel better about your mom's death. It's not that we are braver or stronger, or that your aunt is more emotional. We've had a little more time together to share our sad news and our feelings. Every time you see someone for the first time at the funeral you'll have new feelings. Sometimes we'll be able to comfort that person, sometimes we'll start to cry all over again. We never know which feelings will happen when we see people who mean a lot to us."

Children may be confused by the things people say to them at formal services. Relatives and friends who are somewhat unfamiliar may approach them, hug them, and talk to them with words of endearment. We need to convey to our children that this is the way people reach out and try to help when someone dies. By giving children the words to use when people offer condolences, we let them know that sharing is an important and necessary part of the grieving process.

Offering Condolences

Just as it is uncomfortable to receive words of consolation it is also difficult to find the right words to extend to those who are grieving. Children are puzzled as to what to say, and often they remain silent. We can help our children by giving them the tools to feel more comfortable in these situations. Make sure that the words you suggest are meaningful to your child, simple, and easy to remember. Some examples are:

"I feel so sad that this has happened."
"I feel so bad that your father died."
"I'm really sorry to hear about your father's death."
"I wanted to come here to be with you."

Sometimes children will be quite spontaneous and say things like, "It's just not fair. I don't understand why this had to happen." If your children have a special relationship with a friend who has experienced a loss, it is all right for them to use familiar words to verbalize their frustration or surprise. Remind them to avoid the words, "It must be hard. I know how you feel." This is false reassurance. Unless one has truly experienced a loss yourself in the very same way, you really doesn't know how that friend feels. You can only imagine the pain of loss for that person.

Children may resist visiting a friend or family when there has been a death. They often don't know what to expect and are not sure what to say. We need to let children know that it is perfectly all right to say and do the things they would ordinarily do with their friend. While their activities won't be as animated or as care-free, children need to have visits with friends at times of loss. They don't always have to talk about the person who has died or the feelings and details related to the mourning services. Let your children know that the beginning of the visit is the time to express their feelings of sympathy and to let the griever know how they feel:

"If we don't tell our friends how we feel when we first greet them, it will be harder to say the words later on. There is also the chance that a friend or relative might think we don't want to talk about the person who has died. Let the conversation go from there. Maybe the subject of the death will come up again. It is important not to change the subject. If the death is not talked about again, it doesn't mean that the person doesn't care; he may just not be ready to talk at that time."

Sensitive Answers
to Difficult Questions

What is a wake?

"Some families want to allow everyone the time to pay respects or to visit the family of the person who has died. One way to do this is to have a wake. It usually is held in a funeral home, the special place where people who have died are prepared to be buried or cremated. The casket is in the front of a large room with chairs for the family, friends, and relatives. Visitors come to tell the family how sorry they are that their family member has died. They usually stay for about an hour or so. If the casket is in the front of the room some visitors go to the casket and say a prayer or just remain silent for a moment. If the casket is open, visitors will look at the person and try to remember as much as they can about the person who has died. Sometimes people need to do this several times. It helps us know that the person is really dead."

What happens at a funeral?

"A funeral is a special time when family and friends gather together to publicly share their sadness that a person has died. It is also time for some families to pray together. This can depend on the family's religion. Usually a funeral takes place in a church or a funeral home. There may be a minister, priest, or rabbi to talk about the person who has died and the love and special feelings the family has for this person. Sometimes other people talk about the person who has died. This talk is called a eulogy and mentions important things about the dead person. It often makes other people feel sad. A funeral usually lasts about an hour. After the funeral services the dead person is buried at the cemetery."

Why do I have to go? (Sometimes preceded by "I don't want to go.")

"You really do not *have* to go with us to Grandma's funeral. Your dad and I think that it is very important for all of us to be together at this time, and we would like you to be with us. You don't have to decide right now; you can think about it for a while. You can ask questions. I want you to know that if you feel uncomfortable at the funeral you can sit outside for a short time. Sometimes it's hard to do things like this, and going to a funeral is probably one of the hardest. I can understand how you feel. It's important to remember that everyone you love will be there and we're feeling a bit nervous too. But we'd really like you to be there with us."

If a child is very upset about attending a funeral it is probably wise not to push, but this depends on who has died. When the funeral is for a member of the immediate family you can use gentle persuasion and repeat your explanation several times.

Who will be there?

"There will be lots of people at Grandpa's funeral [wake]. You will know many of them but there will be some who are strangers. These are people that knew Grandpa from work or the community. There will even be some of your grandmother's coworkers and friends. Everyone comes to tell Grandma and the rest of our family how sorry they are that Grandpa has died."

How come the coffin is open? Why do we look at a dead person?

"That is a really good question, and I'm glad you asked. Everyone thinks about the answer to this question. Not all families decide to have an open casket. Some families and religions believe that it is important for everyone to see the person they love dead. It makes the death seem real, instead of just a bad dream. Sometimes when we lose a favorite book or toy we keep hoping to find it and have it back again. It is sort of the same thing when someone dies. If a person has been sick for a long time or has an accident and suddenly dies, that person isn't there anymore for us. If we don't see the person dead we may wish and hope that the person will come back. Seeing a person dead helps us to understand how final death is, and no matter how hard we hope and wish, we won't be able to find that person again.

Lots of times mothers and fathers think that their children shouldn't have to look at a dead person because it might scare them. It might be scary at first but I'll be there with you, and if you don't want to stay by the casket you don't have to."

Why do people laugh and have fun at the party after the funeral?

"This seems very confusing to many of us. The time when a family gathers together after a funeral is a time of relief. There have been long, hard days of grieving and feeling sad. Sometimes it feels good to laugh and smile. For the first few days after the death of a person in the family we haven't smiled very much at all. This doesn't mean we've forgotten about the person who has died; as a matter of fact, we often talk about all the good memories we have of this person."

Why are some people cremated [or burned or turned into ashes] after they die?

"People are not really burned after they die. Cremation is the process of turning a body into ashes. There is no fire but a very high heat that dries out the body. People can choose what they would like to do with their bodies after they die, and some people choose cremation. After the body is turned into ashes, those ashes are put in a special place. For example, people who like the ocean might like their ashes sprinkled over the water. There are people who wish to donate their bodies to science. They leave a special will telling their family that they would like their body given to a medical school or their organs donated to others."

Why are some people put into the ground [or buried] after they die?

"Some people decide they want their bodies to be buried in a cemetery after they die. For many years families have buried mothers, fathers, aunts, and uncles in cemeteries. Burial is a way for us to remember people we love after they have died. The body of a person who has died is put in a special wooden or metal box, called a casket, and placed in a deep opening in the ground. Very often we plant flowers on the ground above the casket. There is usually a stone that marks the grave and tells the person's name, birthday, and date of death. Families visit the cemetery and think about or pray for the person who has died."

3

REENTERING

Getting Back to "Life As Usual"

After the busy-ness of the formal mourning period, families begin to get back to "life as usual." The previous weeks were filled with visits from friends and relatives and a very structured schedule. But of course life is now anything but usual. Your child's daily existence will be changed as a result of the loss he has experienced. If the loss is intimate—a parent, brother, or sister—life will be markedly changed from the first moment in the morning to the last moment at night. Sometimes those changes are even felt during sleep, with dreams constantly reminding young minds of the new pain in their lives. When the loss is more distant—grandparents, classmates, or relatives of friends—the reminders are not as intense. Yet they are still present, always waiting to surface when least expected.

Reentering familiar environments such as school, community activities, play groups, or religious programs can be difficult. While everything seems the same, it really is not. Although children feel good about going back to these "safe" places, they also experience sadness. Children find themselves thinking, "the last time I was here, my brother was alive." Those memories and thoughts are part of the grieving process and can't be avoided, much as we might like to try.

Going back to school is usually the first time children confront reentering. When is the best time for your child to go back to school? One week later? Two weeks later? What can you tell your child to ease the transition? How do we prepare children for the events of the next four to six weeks?

The weeks following the death of someone important in your child's life is filled with daily hurdles and challenges. Children anticipate that "things will be different" but they are not exactly sure how different. They are confused by the new feelings they experience. But as difficult as this time can be, it is also an opportunity for restructuring. There is familiarity and a routine to follow. School can be a haven for children as they concentrate on classwork and momentarily forget the loss. But there may be times during the day when children become engrossed in their thoughts and feel sad. While these occurrences are not unusual, there are things that we as parents can do to help our children ease the reentering process.

Going Back to School

The First Day Back

What is the best time for you to send you child back to school? It is always best to wait until all formal mourning ceremonies or rites have ended. If the death is in the immediate family you may consider a few days of adjustment after the funeral or memorial services conclude. A total time of one week to ten days is about right. To wait longer increases children's feelings of uneasiness regarding the first day back. In addition, children need to be with their friends and classmates. Sometimes the timing of the return to school depends on the day of services. The weekend may be sufficient time to settle in after all activities with relatives and other visitors are over. Monday morning is a natural point of return for all children in the class and your child may feel less conspicuous going back then. However, don't make this decision by yourself. Ask your spouse, another family member, or a trusted friend to concur in your decision. You might even consider asking your children how they feel about returning. Remember not to give total responsibility to your children, however; they will already have enough concerns about returning to school. Pushing for an early return can lead to many difficult moments in the classroom. Children want to be a part of the goings-on at home. You won't spare them any unnecessary pain by sending them to school to avoid the events. If other family members are returning to school or work, consider timing everyone's return simultaneously. The family will then form a natural support group for one another.

Scotti returned to school one week after his sister died. There was no question he was ready. Being in the house with all of those people was beginning to get on his nerves. But somehow when he got to his classroom he wasn't quite as excited. He found himself wondering about how his mother was feeling and even thinking about his baby sister. When he and his mother and father had talked about when he should go back to school, he thought they were babying him . . . he was glad they had decided he should not go back any earlier. That evening at the dinner table Scotti and his parents talked about how they had spent the day and how they all could get through the difficult moments in the days ahead.

Timing is so important to the processing of early griefwork. Premature separation from family can make the burden of loss even heavier.

Mary Beth was not allowed to participate in any of the funeral services for her mother. She was taken to live with another relative the day her mother died, and she started at a new school the next day. Well-meaning aunts and uncles thought it would help her "forget" the sadness. It was not a good year for Mary Beth. She had great difficulty in school and remembers being a behavior problem. Mary Beth went from being an angry eleven-year-old to being an angry teenager. Some thirty-five years later Mary Beth still feels the rage she had for those well-meaning people. It was many years before she could even speak to her family.

Once you've made the decision on timing you will then have to face preparation. How can you help make this experience easier for your children? Is it even possible?

Preparing Your Child for School

Be honest when you talk to your children about going back to school.

"It will be a bit difficult but it will also be good to be back with your teacher and friends. People might ask questions but they can be answered. There will be sad moments but they won't last for a long time and will gradually become less frequent."

There are some little tricks you can use to help soften those moments of sadness. We parents often want to—

and should—let our children know we are thinking of them.

> Kevin returned to school seven days after his grand-mother's death. He had a very close relationship with this grandparent and was feeling a little anxious about going back to school. Kevin's mother spent some time preparing him. While making his lunch for school the next day she packed a short note that said, "Mom and Dad love you very much and we're thinking of you. See you when you get home."

That note was a way of reaching out and letting Kevin touch bases with home during the school day. You may think of other ways to reach out to your children. Listen for clues and try to anticipate their needs. But be sure your messages are subtle, especially for children who are older; a note from Mom might embarrass a son or daughter in the lunchroom.

Remember that preparing children for the first day back at school need not be hours long. You want to give just enough information to ease any anxious feelings. Overloading children by talking about a multitude of possible feelings may only confuse them. Talk to your children several days before they go to school:

> "I'm going back to work on Monday, and I think that might be a good time for you to go to school. We've both had a busy week, but we'll have a few days that will be quieter before you go back to school and I go to work."

Talk to your children once or twice before they actually return to class. The night before is especially important. Support and reassurance will be accepted more readily as the time grows nearer. Share with your children similar situations from your own experience. Discussions such as these usually pave the way for questions that might not otherwise be asked.

When School Is Not in Session

But what if school is not in session? Keep in mind that many of these ideas apply to the first day back to school, whether that is in the middle of the year or at the beginning of the new school year. In both cases, there will be children who know of your child's loss and others who do not. If the death has occurred when school is not in session, you may consider preparing your children for questions from their peers.

The summer and other vacation times may pose more problems for your child, since their lives are less structured and they see less of their classmates and friends. Since the summer doesn't provide the same ready-made social setting as school, you will want to encourage socialization. Call several key friends of your children, or their families. They in turn will move the information through their "network." This is especially important when a child or adolescent has died. Surviving friends need to participate in mourning or acknowledge in some way the loss of their friend. Remember, you are not trying to "keep your children busy" during these nonschool times in order to feel less pain; instead, you are supporting your children in the relationships that are most significant for them. Sharing a lazy summer afternoon with a good friend will do more for a grieving child than an endless string of activities.

Coping With Difficult Moments

Children facing old, familiar situations without their brother, sister, or best friend can be quite upset as they anticipate, then deal with, sad feelings. Difficult times may include walking to school, riding on the school bus, participating in recess activities, or even carpooling. As parents we must prepare ourselves for possible reactions in our children; some children will feel uncomfortable while others may be oblivious to any feelings at all.

Jimmy's bus seat was empty the day after he died. Some of the children knew what had happened but no one was talking about the accident. At one of the last bus stops Nora got on the bus and, noticing the empty seat, asked where Jimmy was. Another student answered, "He's dead." Nora didn't believe the blunt words at first but when others convinced her of the reality of the situation she became very upset. Ryan was also upset; he couldn't believe his brother had been so "mean" as to tell Nora as he did. For weeks no one sat in Jimmy's seat. It was as though all the children wanted to keep a special place in his honor.

We need to prepare our children for these kinds of situations. While we don't want to overemphasize the possible discomfort they may experience, we don't want them to be surprised either. A matter-of-fact approach usually works best.

"There will be times during the school day that you'll really miss Jimmy. You might feel sad or you might even feel angry that he isn't there to be with you."

Reassure your child that these feelings are normal and will become less frequent as time passes. The first time is always the hardest.

Talking to the Teacher

One way to ensure that you will know how your children are coping with school is to establish a channel of communication with their teachers. An informed teacher is your children's best asset during school hours. Many people feel that it isn't essential that the teacher know what has happened in your children's life, or needs, at the most, only scanty details about the loss. However, an informed teacher has greater awareness of children's needs in the classroom. Some teachers are very perceptive and can spot children in distress, but it makes more sense to let an educator know of your children's particular situation at once.

You can begin by telling the teacher who has died and your children's relationship to that person. Other important points to share are your children's response to the circumstances of the death, their exact understanding of the death, and their involvement in and reaction to funeral or memorial services. Knowledge of these circumstances helps the teacher interpret your children's behavior in context and dispel any misinformation on the part of other students. Children tend to be blunt with each other. The teacher who is kept informed can help ease some otherwise tense times.

Talk to the teacher frequently. Offer to receive calls. Share new information with your child's educator as necessary—probably once each week during the first six weeks is sufficient. By keeping the lines of communication open you will know immediately if there is a problem. More likely, you will feel reassured that your children are returning to their old routines.

Talking to Friends

We all know that children are usually very direct with each other. Sometimes they even seem cruel as they verbalize uncensored thoughts to their friends. Children occasionally perceive the words of their friends in response to a death in their family as harsh and uncaring.

One father told me that his seven-year-old daughter was ostracized by her friends because she did not have a mother.

Maggie was treated differently not only by her own peers in the third grade, but also by the parents of these friends. Sensing this strain in her relationships with others, Maggie withdrew. Maggie's father thought that the teasing was perceived by his daughter as an attack and didn't know how to handle this very confusing situation. Here were her so-called friends, making her feel worse at a time when she was already experiencing tremendous pain. But all was not doom and gloom. Maggie had a crew of "protectors." Other girls in her class would defend Maggie whenever necessary.

Maggie's father was supportive and encouraged his daughter to be forgiving. He further explained how important it is to respect others. He summed up his thoughts with the following words:

"Your friends don't do things to be mean, even though it hurts. Sometimes people don't know what to do in these situations. They are confused, and we have to understand that."

We can help our children navigate these troubled waters in their relationships by giving them support each time they are confronted with perplexing situations. Younger children, particularly, do not hesitate to speak their minds. This can result in very uncomfortable and even angry moments among friends. Older children are very much aware that they may say the wrong thing and often do not say anything at all. Grieving children believe that their quiet friends just don't care, that their outspoken friends are callous. As parents we want to shield our children from further pain. We may feel angry when hurtful remarks are directed toward them, or when they feel shunned. We have to remember the words spoken by Maggie's father: The hurt those words carry is not intentional; it is the result of people being uncomfortable.

Daily Challenges

When we anticipate the big events in life, we gear up and brace ourselves for what we are about to experience. When someone dies, these are the big moments: visiting the grave for the first time, going to the funeral home, going back to work or school. But it is the little things that often throw us—and when we least expect it. The next section will focus on the so-called little things, and how to deal with them when they occur in our children's lives.

Telephone Calls and Mail

Answering the telephone seems harmless enough, but for a child who has recently had a loss, particularly the loss of a parent, a phone call can be an unsettling situation.

Maggie and Allison came home after school every day to an empty house. Their mother had died five weeks earlier and the girls were by themselves until their father came home from work two hours later. The phone would ring several times during those hours. Usually it was a friend calling, but on more than one occasion it was a stranger asking for the "Mrs." or requesting to speak to the girls' mother. If the girls told the caller "She's not here," they were pressed for the time of her return. One day after several frustrating exchanges Maggie tearfully blurted out, "She's dead!"

Allison and Maggie's father reported several difficult months coping with this problem. At one point the girls would simply slam the phone down if anyone called for their mother. It took time for his daughters to heed his gentle guidance. A year and a half later he acknowledged that the girls had absolutely no hesitation in telling an unknown caller that their mother was dead. As a matter of fact, he thought they were now a bit *too* willing to do so. (At times children may experience a sort of satisfaction when callers are rendered speechless and suddenly hang up.)

Receiving mail is another potentially upsetting dilemma. One mother told me that her son had been dead for only two weeks when his tickets for a spring vacation arrived at her home. His twin brother also received his tickets the same day. The mother said with tears, "How can I take each day as it comes when there are constant reminders of what the future was to bring for my son?" Children can have the same feelings of anger and sadness when a letter comes addressed to the one who has died. Children are curious and want to open the letters. They also know that they will stir up feelings of grief. Their reactions to this conflict can range from indifference to out-and-out avoidance of the mailbox. Whether it is the telephone or the mail, you need to remember that their reactions are temporary. They are adjusting to the newness of the situation. Let your children decide what they would like to do. An answering machine may be a solution. Leaving the mail on the hall table until an adult gets home is not going to cause great difficulty. The best approach is to talk about the possibility of these events happening before they occur. Tell your children that these kinds of things can happen to them. Talk about ways to handle those times. You might even consider role playing to help your children feel more comfortable. You may feel more comfortable as well.

Seeing Old (and Meeting New) Acquaintances

It is almost inevitable: Sooner or later your child will meet a friend or teacher or community member who has not heard the news of the loss in your child's life. Someone will ask, "By the way, how are your parents?" or say, "Ask your mother if you can come over after school." Children will be overwhelmed in these situations because they expect that everyone should know about the tragedy in their lives. Being confronted with someone who does not know about the loss is like pouring salt in a wound that is just beginning to heal. Suddenly, when least expected, your child will have to answer this question honestly. The truth of that moment is difficult enough to handle—but children will also have to deal with an adult or another child who will feel embarrassed and saddened at having been so "thoughtless."

Eight-year-old Cindy was in the grocery store with her mother only five weeks after her ten-year-old

sister Shannon had died quite suddenly. At the
checkout counter Cindy saw a girl who was in Shannon's Girl Scout troop. The old friend had moved
the year before and was back in town visiting her
grandmother. In horror Cindy knew what would
happen next. "How's Shannon? Tell her I said hi!"
Unable to tell the truth and risk tears in this very
public setting. Cindy weakly answered "Oh, she's
fine; I'll let her know."

It is impossible to eradicate these painful moments
from our children's lives but we can prepare them. In
addition, we can help them to answer the questions of
others gracefully and with some degree of comfort.

First of all, tell your children early in the reentering
phase that these things *will* happen—maybe not the
first week, or the second, but in time. Second, give your
children the means to share the news in an honest way.
You may even role play with your children to help them
practice. Give them several short, easy-to-remember
phrases:

"I'm sorry to tell you but my sister died last month."
"It's hard for me to tell you this but my brother
died six months ago."

Of course, people will want to know what happened,
but it's not necessary for your children to go into the
details unless they want to.

Next, prepare your children for the responses they are
likely to hear: "Oh, I'm so sorry, I didn't know" or "Oh,
you poor thing. And I was so thoughtless." Tell your
children that people in these situations will be very
embarrassed and upset but that is not anyone's fault.
Their friends or acquaintances are not being thoughtless or cruel, because they had no idea there had been a

loss. Under these circumstances people may become very quiet or leave hurriedly. Tell your child that people act this way because they are uncomfortable, not because they don't care.

Social Activities

After-school and other social events play a critical role in children's lives. They see their friends, have fun, and let go. There is no secret formula for knowing the best time to resume these activities after a death. Some events may be very comfortable for children; others may provoke anxiety. You need to evaluate each activity separately. Don't assume that because your child had a good time at Scouts he will also enjoy the soccer game. Events in our children's lives have different meanings. They are colored by the people involved and by individual preferences.

Scouts, Religious School, Sports, and Community Activities

There are times and activities when children are accompanied by their parents: Mothers may be Brownie and Girl Scout leaders; fathers may go on campouts with their sons; both parents may attend special functions and watch children at soccer games, wrestling matches, and other sports. The first time your child goes back to any of these activities it will be with some feeling of anxiety. Children worry that they are going to be different from others.

One way to alleviate some of those fears is to make plans ahead of time. By preparing for these events you give your children a way of participating in the decision on how to handle these events. You can begin by asking who they would like to have in Dad's or Mother's place. Tell them that at first the activity will be a little different but that they will feel more comfortable with time. Remember that these feelings are temporary and are less disruptive than ending the activity altogether would be. Community and after-school activities provide a sense of familiarity and comfort. In a world that has been turned upside down, a Scout meeting or baseball game can be a temporary oasis.

As the surviving parent we often feel we have to be den mother, coach, teacher, and cheerleader. But there are friends, relatives, neighbors, and other parents who are often eager to help. Let them. There is nothing to be gained, except exhaustion, if we try to do it all.

When Your Child "Doesn't Want to Do Anything"

After making all the arrangements for your children to go to their various activities, they may decide that they just can't go—usually at the last minute. What do you do? Urge and coax? Or let them stay home? Each situation is different. It is wise to keep several things in mind as you make the decision. Weigh carefully who will be there and your children's feelings about the activity before the loss. If your daughter couldn't stand Bible school before her mother died and tells you she just can't go because she'll be too upset, chances are feelings of grief are compounding those other feelings. "Tease out" what is really going on. On the other hand, if wrestling was an all-time favorite with your son and he decides he just can't go because his dad won't be there to root for him, you can help him talk about his thoughts and reassure him that you or another adult will be there to cheer him on.

Preparing children for their feelings is the key. Let them know they will feel like staying home. It may seem easier not to go, but it won't be any easier the second, third, and fourth times. You might tell your children, "Hold your nose and jump in!" Follow words of encouragement with the reassurance that if they really don't want to stay after they get to Scouts, they can call you or another person. Be sure you have a plan to allow for the possibility of their calling. Occasionally, after several weeks, you children may be having a bad day—those are allowed! Staying home that day may help. Try to be flexible but not so much that your children, rather than you, are deciding what's best for them.

When Children Ask About Possessions

Toward the end of the first four to six weeks after a family member dies, children will begin to think about the possessions of that person. Some children may ask what the parent is going to do with their grandmother's clothes or their sister's toys. There is no rush to decide what to do with these things. You must feel comfortable with your decisions on when and to whom you will give the belongings of the person who has died. Children may urge you to take action. Don't do it unless you are ready. Tell your children that you will know when the time is right. One day it will just happen.

Often families worry about how to handle these times. The time to take action is when it "feels right." Of course, some people are eager to remove all possessions immediately. I put the brakes on these families; griefwork can't be hurried by changing the environment. Children need to understand this as well. Explain to your children that having these reminders around can help us grieve. When we see the clothes, toys, or other belongings of someone who has died, we think of that person. At the beginning the thoughts will make us feel sad. After a while the thoughts will be warm and comforting. One young mother told me about the time she reached into her coat pocket and found a small pink barrette. She smiled to herself as she thought of the infant daughter who had died six month earlier. Those feelings are bittersweet, a mixture of comfort and sadness at the same time. Nevertheless, they are a necessary part of the grieving process. Tell your children about these strange feelings. They will be less confused when they experience them for the first time.

Helping Your Child Move Through Griefwork

What is this process of grieving? What is the behavior you can expect to see in your children? How do you know if they are "on course"? Questions like these will pass through your mind from time to time in the early weeks after a loss. It is natural to wonder how your child is doing, but because children do not mourn in the same manner as adults we cannot predict a sequence of stages.

Robby was eighteen years old when he was killed in a car accident. Surviving him were his parents, a twin brother, a sixteen-year-old sister and an eight-year-old brother. His mother became distraught when she compared the behavior of her children.

Robby's twin was robotlike, constantly on the go and trying to put the tragedy out of his mind. Glenna, the sixteen-year-old, was having a very difficult time. She frequently cried, wrote letters to her parents, and talked about Robby. Adam, the youngest, had no apparent behavioral changes. His mother described him as "not sensing the danger" as much as the other children. She was frantically trying to assess which child was in trouble because of not coping. She wanted to know if she should seek professional help for her children. But her biggest concern centered on how she should help her children grieve and talk to her about their feelings.

Each child grieves in a different way. Some are very demonstrative, while others keep their grief as a very private experience. Some children appear not to be grieving at all. Which of these children are doing their griefwork? All of them, each in an individual way.

Robby's mother was anticipating psychological problems only six weeks after the loss of her son. You can expect griefwork to continue for at least a year, and usually longer. Don't try to diagnose problems with your children at an early point. Give them time. Consider their personalities and how they may influence grieving. Age is another important factor. Younger children may not verbalize their feelings as older children do; instead they "play out" their feelings. As in Adam's case, younger children may appear to be oblivious to loss in the family.

Allow your children to express themselves their own way. View new and different behaviors as "symptoms" of grieving. Respond to your children's actions by talking about the loss, *not* about the behavior itself. The chances are your children may not know that their behavior is related to the loss in their lives. When your children are having difficult times—acting out in school, having crying spells at bedtime, or making visits to the school nurse—talk about the feelings that come with grief.

When I talk with children I sometimes use the analogy of physical symptoms.

"When you have an infection inside of your body, you don't always know about it; you might have a fever or a sore throat. These things tell us we have to pay attention to what is going on inside of our body and try to make it better—by staying warm, drinking lots of juices, or even visiting the doctor. When someone we love dies there is also something going on inside of us. It's not a sickness, but like a sore it takes time to heal and get better.

"Many people don't recognize the soreness of grief because the signs are different than a sore throat or a fever: some children don't sleep very well, some feel very sad, some even get into trouble in school. Of course, there isn't a special medicine to take or juices to drink to make that pain go away. Time is the best medicine, much as it is with a cut that has to heal. But grieving takes longer. We can help ourselves feel better by talking to other people. We feel sad when we think about the person who has died. But those thoughts help heal our pain when we share them with other people."

Talking to your Child

Talking to your children about loss can be difficult, especially when they ask questions. Listen for clues in your day-to-day conversations with them. Children have a way of slipping out a word or two when we least expect it. Take time to pick up on their hints. A casual comment is often a test to see if we are listening to their words. Your response can be very simple. "Gee, it sounds like you have been thinking about your grandma." You don't always have to initiate dialogue with your children. Listen carefully and facilitate their talks with you.

Be honest with your own feelings in front of your children. If you maintain a "strong" image for them, they might try to do the same for you. Children will be puzzled if they never see you cry or show your sadness. They may even think that you don't care. Sometimes children see their parents cry and feel responsible for making them upset. Be sure to tell them that feeling sad is part of grieving; emphasize the fact that they didn't cause you to cry. Sharing feelings with your children is an enriching experience for both of you. You will find that your burden of loss will be lightened as well.

Sensitive Answers to Difficult Questions

Most of the difficult questions and situations your children may have at this time revolve around other people in their lives being unaware of their loss. There are many situations when they will have to acknowledge the death of the person they love. It might seem easier to ignore it or deny that the death has occurred, but eventually everyone has to come to terms with the loss.

You may want to use the following questions and sample answers in your own situation. The answers may not be totally appropriate for your children; substitute your own words and make them fit. Some children don't seem to want to know anything; they rarely ask questions and shy away if you approach them. You might use these questions to initiate discussion with your children saying, "Does anything like this ever come to your mind?" By doing this you let your children know that it is okay to inquire about the things that concern them. You also let them know that you are aware of their concerns. If it's an issue for them, they will listen; if it's not, no harm has been done. You will not frighten them or put ideas into their heads. The chances are your children have already thought of these questions and are relieved to find that you know what might be upsetting them.

What happens when I go to school for the first time? What will I say?

"When you return to school after this week there will be times that will be difficult for you. You might find yourself thinking of Grandma during the day. You will feel sad and it might be hard to think about your schoolwork. Those moments won't last a long time at all. One or two minutes, maybe a bit longer. You'll get back to your schoolwork. At first those times will happen a lot, gradually you'll find that they will happen less frequently.

"People may not know what to say to you so you have to help them understand how you feel. Some children may come up to you and say "I'm sorry about what happened." Some may not know what to say at all. This doesn't mean that they don't care; it means that they just can't find the right words. Eventually your friends will find those special words to tell you how they feel and that will make you feel good."

What happens if I start to cry in school?

"If you feel upset in school and start to cry, ask the teacher if you can leave the room for a few minutes. I will have already talked to her, and she will understand. This is very natural and normal for anyone who has lost someone that they love. During the day I even have times when I feel sad and I just have to sit down and cry. This is all part of grieving and actually helps us to feel better about losing Grandma.

"If you feel especially sad and want to talk to someone, you can always call me from school. I'll make sure that you always have money for the school telephone. If you want you can even talk to [here you can mention a favorite teacher, the school nurse, or another caring adult]. Sharing our thoughts with other people helps us to feel better. Grieving is like carrying a heavy load; when we share our feelings, someone else helps us to carry that load—it's just a bit easier for us."

What do I say when other kids ask me what happened?

"Sometimes other children are just curious and want to know why you have been absent from school. The people in your class will know because we've told your teacher. She will explain to your classmates what has happened. Sometimes children in other classes will ask you questions. The best thing I can tell you is to say, 'My grandmother died and I stayed home for a week to be with my family.'

"It might seem that other children won't know

what to do when you tell them. This doesn't mean
you shouldn't tell them. Chances are sooner or later
someone will ask and you may as well be honest.
Always be truthful about what has happened. It is
much easier than trying to remember different
stories."

When I went to the mailbox today and saw a letter for Mom, I started to cry. I don't want to ever look at the mail anymore.

"There will always be reminders of Mom and it's
not going to be easy. Sometimes it might be a letter
in the mailbox, sometimes a favorite program of
hers on TV, or maybe even a telephone call. We
can't run away, even though we would like to. Whenever we face these reminders we feel sad for a few
minutes. Time will make us feel better and we will
gradually feel more comfortable when these things
happen. But if you really don't want to look at the
mail right now, that's okay too."

What do I say when someone calls and asks to talk to my mother? If I say she's not home, the person asks what time she'll be back.

"This is a tough situation. Many children with
only one parent at home have the same problem.
We're going to work out something for you to say.
We can even write it on a piece of paper and leave
it right next to the telephone. Some answers you
could use are: 'Only my father lives here,' and 'My

father is busy right now; please call back later.'
You don't have to tell every person who calls that
your mother has died, but you do have to let them
know that your father is the person to speak to.
Being honest is the best approach. If you say 'My
mother is busy now,' the person will want to know
more. If you let them know that your father is the
person to talk to, they can ask about your father."

What will I do when it's Mother's Day or Christmas or Hanukkah? Everyone else will be making presents for their mothers and I won't.

"These occasions are very hard for us because they
remind us how much we miss Mom. But that doesn't
mean that you can't participate with the rest of the
class. You'll make your gift or card for a different
person. On Mother's Day you can make your present for Grandma [or another favorite female person];
on other holidays you can make things for other
people in our family. You can still do what everyone else is doing, but your gift will go to a special
person you've chosen instead of Mom."

Who will go with me to Scout meetings now that Dad isn't here?

"Let's talk about that. I'm really glad you asked me
because I've been thinking about it myself. Do you
think you'd like to have someone else in Dad's place?
It might be nice to have someone there. It won't be
the same but it sure will help you feel a bit more
comfortable. Is there another father at the meeting,

maybe one of your friend's dads, who can help?
Why don't we talk to him?"

Although it may seem that you are giving your child
a lot of responsibility in this situation, you're really not.
Before this conversation takes place, you need to explore
possibilities for companionship. Don't make the decision
first. Giving your child a sense of control will ease the
transition.

Who will walk to school with me now that Jimmy has died?

"I know that you're really going to miss Jimmy
many times during the day. He was your best friend.
Let's talk about ways that you might feel better
walking to school. What would you like to do?"

Explore options with your child: walking with another
person, a brother, or sister. Sometimes children will
want you to "fix" their feelings and ask you to take
them to school. This is not a long-term solution and
you'll still be faced with the same problem in a few
weeks. If you do feel that your child would benefit from
a drive to school, be sure to set a time limit and then
stick to it.

Who will I have to talk to at night when I go to sleep? I'll be lonely.

"This is another one of those times when it is very
hard to make changes and get used to the fact that
your brother is no longer here. Mom and Dad will
come in and talk to you at night and stay with you

a little while to help you get to sleep. We can talk about how you feel and any loneliness you might have. We can also try some other things before you go to sleep; maybe you'd like to listen to a record or read a favorite story. What do you think you'd like to do? It will be harder in the beginning to fall asleep. You'll have lots of thoughts in your head. After a while falling asleep will be easier, although you will probably feel sad when you think about your brother. Those sad times will gradually go away—it just takes time."

4

A YEAR OF FIRSTS

Helping Your Children
Through the First Year

This first year is a time of ups and downs for both you and your children. Inevitably, just when the pain seems to be lessening there is some new reminder of the person who is so missed. Feelings of loss resurface nearly as strong as before. The first year following a loss is filled with memories and experiences new to children and their parents—the first Christmas or Yom Kippur, the birthday or wedding anniversary of the person who has died, the changing seasons. Each situation is new because it is the first time family or friends must face the loss on that particular occasion. You need to learn how to help your children approach holidays and other events.

Adjustment

Following the time of reentry, families move through a period of adjustment. Some researchers say this period lasts about one year; most families, however, find that the time is really closer to two or three years. During that first year we adjust to the loss in our lives. Although we never really accept death we try to live without the person in our day-to-day activities. But the pain does not completely go away. Grieving, finally, is not a process of acceptance but of integration—we take in, or integrate, the loss of our family member or friend into our lives.

We don't know how long it takes children to adjust to loss, although it is probably somewhat longer than the time period needed by adults. This should not surprise us. After all, when children experience a death they lose the opportunity to develop a relationship with the person who has died; in many cases adults have already established that relationship. Then, too, adults have shared many of life's important events with the person who is dead; children must face those events with a piece missing. So it is very important that your child's first year of loss be a strong foundation for the years ahead.

The Early Months

The early months after your child experiences a loss are a time of major life changes. If you have lost a member of your immediate family everyone will struggle with these experiences in a profound way. If your child has lost a friend, classmate, or teacher you may not feel the event with the same emotional intensity as your child. Nevertheless everyone in the family will have to cope with the changes in some way.

Sameness and Stability

If at all possible, don't make any other changes in your life during the early months of griefwork; if you can, wait at least one year. Some people believe that they can move on and grieve faster if they make changes in another part of their lives, hoping to keep busy and thus diminish the pain of their loss. Actually, griefwork is compounded and slowed tremendously when we start to cope with additional stresses or changes. Even positive changes will still have to be worked through.

Vanessa lost her best friend in the fifth grade. She wandered about aimlessly for the first few weeks after she returned to school. Her parents, sensing her pain, decided that if they changed her school she would not experience the daily reminders of her friend's death. Vanessa's mourning exploded into anger and rage. She now had to cope with the loss of her friend, plus that of her school and her classmates. A very stable and structured part of her life had been removed and she reacted with great intensity. After consultation with the school guidance counselor Vanessa was returned to her original school and the support of her friends.

Vanessa's parents did not think they would harm their daughter by sending her to a new school, they wanted desperately to spare her the anguish of grief. Instead, they added to the work to be done. Other changes to be avoided are moving, remarrying, divorcing, changing child-care arrangements, or changing jobs. Sometimes, of course, there may be no other alternative for you. Remember that you and your children will have to deal with several losses at the same time. Provide sameness and stability in as many areas of your child's life as possible. Predictable routines and a stable environment are key components for griefwork in those first six months; there is great comfort knowing that you will have the same house and same teachers when the rest of your life is in turmoil.

New Traditions for Meaningful Times

Perhaps important holidays are the most feared events in the first year after the loss of a family member or friend. No matter what time of year a death occurs people immediately think of that first Christmas, Passover, or New Year. While children do not project into the future as much as adults, those times are just as difficult for them. The difference is that adults will usually talk about their fears while children will not.

We can't remove the holidays from the calendar or ignore their existence, much as we might like to. We have to prepare as best we can for the emotional peaks and valleys we will experience at these significant times. While we adults tend to feel intense sadness throughout these occasions, children seem to be able to more clearly separate the joy of the holiday from the grief of loss.

Jim's wife died ten months before Christmas, and he knew that the holidays would be hard for him and his children. He described his emotions: "I didn't think it would be too bad, but I found out it was *really bad*. I felt no joy whatsoever. I just wanted the days to go by quickly." Jim's two daughters, seven and ten years of age, felt sadness on Christmas Eve but appeared to enjoy the holiday when they joined cousins and other family members.

Part of the problem in determining how children are coping is that they often *appear* to be untouched by grief. We look at children when they appear to be happy and wonder what they are really thinking. Unlike adults, who grieve publicly and articulately, children's emotions are worked out in other ways. Sometimes they may even put their feelings on hold for the time being.

It is often easier for us to accept what we see in our children than to question; we fear we will upset them with our own feelings. What can we do to make important family occasions less fraught with sadness? Should we let our children experience the joy without addressing the loss in their lives?

Try not to overcompensate for the loss with gifts and special treats for your children. Nothing can replace the loss in their lives. Children need extra time and attention on these occasions, not extra things. One mother explained to me that she thought her son was "doing fine" after her husband's death. "He was so busy with all of his toys he didn't seem to be upset at all." Sometimes a parent's perception of a child who is "doing fine" will serve to make communication even more difficult, and as a result, each feels more alone.

Don't try to change or diminish holiday celebrations. Granted, a holiday in the first year after the loss of a family member may not be a very joyous occasion, but altering traditional family celebrations will compound the sadness your child will experience. Instead of celebrating differently, add a new custom or tradition to commemorate the person who has died: a special prayer, a poetry reading, a visit to the grave, a donation of time or services to a charity. Encourage your children to think about what they might like to do; ask for their suggestions. These activities give holidays and religious celebrations a new meaning and expand the traditional customs of those occasions.

Gerry was ten years old when his father was suddenly killed in a freak accident at work only eight weeks before Christmas. His mother wondered how she would get through the holidays with her young son. She decided to keep the family's celebration intact. In addition, the family would visit their father's grave in the morning and bring a basket of cookies to the senior citizen's center. The children made all the decisions for this new tradition, which was carried out every year after that.

A new tradition will not only be meaningful to the family by commemorating the life of the person who has died; it will also provide an opportunity for everyone in the family to share their feelings.

Trying to Understand "Different" Behavior

One of the most challenging aspects of childhood grief is the new and unexpected behavior exhibited by the younger members of your family. Children who were calm and good-natured become surly and overactive. Little irritations become major catastrophes; tears and wailing are commonplace. Other children may be very quiet, uninterested in life, almost depressed in their mood.

What can you do about these sudden changes in character? First of all, don't view this behavior as a new problem that compounds your griefwork. These changes are *symptoms* of your child's griefwork. What we verbalize, children act out. Sometimes their behavior is in response to their understanding of events.

Three months after her mother died, five-year-old Susan announced to her father that she too was going to die. She was going to take her own life so she could be with her mother. Susan's father immediately called the community mental health center. He told the professionals there that his daughter was threatening suicide. After several sessions Susan's motives were clear to the professionals who talked with her. Susan used a five-year-old's logic: "My Mom is in heaven, I am here. She's sad and I'm sad. I'll be happy and Mom will be happy if I'm in heaven with her. I have to die to be with Mom." To Susan everything seemed very logical. She was more concerned with reuniting with her mother in a place called heaven than with dying.

The important point to remember for situations like these is to seek help immediately if you are uncomfortable with your child's behavior. You may not be as objective as others. One mother described to me her own feelings of suicide after her ten-year-old died. She knew that she would never act on her feelings, but a five-year-old would not be able to separate reality from wishful thinking.

What about nightmares or dreams when children resurrect the person who has died? They do not mean that your child is not working through his grief. In fact, talking about dreams and their meaning can help you and your child share feelings that might otherwise not be expressed. Children are very intuitive; their dreams may relate thoughts that may surprise or shock us.

Chris was eleven years old when he lost his best friend. They had been virtually inseparable in school and during play. Chris would periodically tell his mother about his dreams regarding his dead friend. One dream in particular was startling to his mother. Chris "saw" Jimmy come to him at night. "It was so real, it felt like he was really there. We had a long talk. I told him I really missed him; I had a lot of things to tell him."

Chris talked about his dream with his mother. Instead of focusing on the unlikelihood of Chris's friend actually being in the bedroom she asked him to talk about his reaction to the dream, how he felt afterward, and what he thought it meant. Chris felt he had unfinished business with his friend. His dream gave him the chance to say what he needed to—a very important part of his griefwork.

Sometimes our children behave in ways that provoke an angry response from us. They can be demanding of our attention, moody, sullen, or clinging. Very young children may regress to earlier stages of development. It is difficult to be sensitive and caring when we are stretched to the limits of our patience. But becoming angry will not help the behavior disappear. Rather, it will only serve to distance your child from you further. Respond to those kinds of behaviors as symptoms of grieving. They are signs of griefwork, not the results of it. When your child begins to act out in any one of these ways, it may help to say to yourself, "He is grieving. He misses his [mother, father, sibling, grandparent, etc.]. He is not doing these things intentionally. He does them because he does not know how to put his feelings into words." You can help your child express his emotions instead of putting his energy into disruptive behaviors. When he demonstrates such symptoms of grief, be very direct. Say, "It must be hard for you now that Dad is gone. I bet you're missing him a lot. I miss him, too." Give an opening for discussion by letting your child know that you know how he is feeling. Don't worry about putting ideas into your children's heads by offering such pointed openers. If your children do have those thoughts your words will reassure them. If they don't have those thoughts, they will let you know. You can usually tell when you're right.

Making Sense Out of Feelings

What can you expect your child to feel during a time of grief? Children experience all of the same feelings that adults do, sometimes more intensely, sometimes less intensely. Remember that we are all entitled to our feelings; they are not right or wrong, good or bad—they just *are*. Telling your children this will help them appreciate that people can feel differently at different times.

While they experience the same emotions as adults, children experience the emotions of grief in a different way. Adults try to talk about feelings; children often act them out. Children seem to bounce back from their sad times faster than adults; they may still feel sad but don't seem to show it as much. We can tell when our children are sad—they stare off into the distance, their eyes look sad, and they're quieter than usual. They might cry or try to hold back their tears with a quivering lip. If we ask what's wrong we get the traditional response: "Nothing." If we ask the question in a different way we may get a different answer. Start conversations with an observation or an open-ended question that needs more than a yes or no answer: "What are you thinking about?" "Tell me your thoughts," or "You look sad. What's going on inside?" Once you get started, keep the dialogue going with cues such as "tell me more," "go on," "um-hmm," or "me, too."

Sharing your own feelings, especially those from your own childhood days, often stimulates more participation. Upon hearing that his mother had feelings similar to his own one little boy simply said "Gee, I guess it runs in the family!" Ask open-ended questions when your child seems to be feeling sad, angry, frustrated, or even happy. The questions will help you find out what's going on inside.

You may not think that feeling good would be a problem, but sometimes parents are upset when their children seem to be doing so well with grief. We expect our children to behave and feel one way and they surprise us with totally different feelings.

Seven months after his wife died, Fred was puzzled by his children's happy dispositions. They were doing well in school and seemed to be enjoying life. He couldn't imagine why they were so "up" when he felt terrible most of the time. He tried to talk about their mother but they weren't interested. He was a bit resentful that they looked so happy. Finally he told his children how he felt. Their explanation was simple; they had felt sad for so long while their mother was sick that they had "used it all up."

It's a good thing we all don't feel the same way at the same time. Parents feel sad and children feel good; children feel sad and their parents feel good. Unfortunately, however, guilty feelings may surface when we do feel better and others do not. Children are somewhat freer than adults when they are having a good time; they don't hesitate to laugh and carry on. But soon there is a reminder of the loss, and they react as if they have done something wrong by enjoying life. We have to tell our children that it is all right to have happy feelings. Not everyone is going to feel good at the same time. Good feelings should be enjoyed; there will also be times for the sad feelings.

The opposite situation can also occur: Your child is feeling sad and lonely but you are having a good day. Suddenly you notice anger or resentment directed toward you. This is quite natural. Children may think, or even say, "How can you be having such a good time when I feel so terrible?" They may even interpret your behavior, or that of others as uncaring.

> Ryan, a twelve-year-old, told his mother that his teacher's mother had died. The teacher was absent for three days. Upon her return all of the students watched her behavior carefully. Ryan's mother asked if he had expressed condolences to the teacher. He replied nonchalantly, "No, she was fine. She didn't look any different than usual. She acted the same way, and besides, she didn't mention it!"

Explain to your children that everyone has their ups and downs during the months of grief. Feeling happy doesn't mean you care less or have forgotten about the person who has died. Our moods can change quickly during the early months of griefwork, with the happy times gradually outnumbering the sad times. But don't tell your children that they shouldn't feel angry. They need to know that anger is acceptable and that others have the same feelings.

Often our children seem depressed as griefwork progresses. It is sometimes difficult to tell the difference between mourning and depression. The early months of the first year are almost too soon to tell; you are more likely to see depression in later months and years. But keep these points in mind.

A child who is *depressed*	A child who is *grieving*
• feels sadness mixed with anger, sometimes directed toward himself	• feels sadness but can switch to more normal moods in the same day

A child who is *depressed*	A child who is *grieving*
• may consistently feel tired, lose his appetite, or have trouble sleeping; may be hyperactive or aggressive (masking depression)	• has changeable moods, activity levels, appetite and sleep patterns
• expresses anger in the form of rage or denies being angry altogether	• expresses anger at appropriate times even if not in appropriate ways
• may not recall dreams, and fantasizes infrequently	• dreams and fantasizes, particularly about the loss
• may see herself as bad and worthless; is preoccupied with herself	• may blame herself for somehow not preventing the death, is preoccupied with the loss
• may be unresponsive to others or responds to pressure and urging	• responds to warmth and reassurance
• is rarely able to enjoy pleasure	• is able to experience pleasure at varying times

Consider also your responses: If your child is grieving, you will feel sympathetic and want to reach out to him. If he is depressed, you may feel irritated, frustrated, or helpless.

Obviously you should not assume that your child is depressed if he shows only one or two signs of depression. Grief takes many forms, and children are far more spontaneous and dramatic than adults. Use these lists as a guideline rather than as a diagnostic tool. You yourself will have a strong sense of how your child is doing. A great deal depends on your child's personality before the loss and what has happened since, in the family and in other parts of his life. Listen to your instincts; parents usually know best.

After a loss, all children experience intense feelings of separation, with a yearning or longing for the person who died. It seems to occur more frequently in the early months but resurfaces again in later years.

> Brent and his brother John were only two years apart in age; they had been involved in many of the same activities and sports, including wrestling. John accidentally died three years ago. In the early months of the first year after John's death Brent missed his older brother sorely. The wrestling season began two weeks after John's death. When the wrestling season opens each year, Brent experiences great yearning for his brother.

No matter what behavior your children exhibit after a loss, remember: it is most likely temporary. Your children will probably not require the services of a psychiatrist. However, you may feel more taxed by their exasperating antics than you realize. Get support for yourself; talk to your children's teachers and others if necessary. Try to focus on the fact that these changes are symptoms of grieving, not permanent personality changes resulting from the loss of someone close to your children. Be patient; talk to your children about their underlying feelings of grief. If, after several months of efforts on your part, your children are still behaving uncharacteristically, in ways that are problematic in the family or at school, consider talking to a counselor. (See Chapter 7, *Getting Help*.)

Little Reminders

How unprepared we are when without warning something crops up in our day-to-day lives that brings back the painful truth—we have lost someone close to us, and it has left a wound on our souls. The pain comes rushing back. As we move into the final months of that first year we try to put our lives in perspective. Then, just when we think we are in control there is some little reminder of the person we miss so dearly. A good example of such little reminders is the roll of film that sits in the camera for almost a year. Six or eight months after a death in the family we finally get the film developed. We look at the pictures in the middle of the film shop and there in living color is Grandma. The shock is unnerving. But we often face these events with a warm remembrance as well as sadness.

Preparing our children for these surprise occurrences is important. No matter how much we tell them however, they will still feel the surprise when it happens to them: A brother's book long overdue at the library, a card from the dentist's office for a sister's yearly checkup, or a friend's secret treasures found at the bottom of the dresser drawer trigger sadness at the loss. Tell your children that these surprises will happen to them when they least expect them. They can't be avoided, and we can't run away. But we can learn from these times. And what we learn is that we can never accept the death of someone we love. We can only get used to it. Not only do these events remind us of the person who is dead, they also remind us to do more griefwork. Perhaps our work is never done.

Remembering

Paul had a difficult task ahead of him. His young wife had died after a long fight against cancer, and now he had to help his three young children, aged six, four, and one, with their grief. Not only would they have to deal with a very deep loss, but they would also have to work hard to remember their mother. About three months after his wife's death, Paul contacted a play therapist.

Memories grow faint when a child experiences a loss at an early age. It is important for children to hold onto the image of a parent, sibling, friend, or relative; if they don't remember the feelings they had for this person, griefwork will be more difficult in later years. Sally Reed, a play therapist with a background in child development, helped the three children mentioned above with a practical yet sensitive approach. She suggested that two older children make a special book remembering their mom. She left the decision to them, and at his own pace each began to create "My Remembering Mommy Book." At first there were discussions on colors, titles, decorations, and drawings. Each book emerged as a personal statement. The books grew rapidly with letters, drawings, and photographs. I recently read through the books with both children. They talked about their mother, the contents of the book, and how they decided to include each piece. The boys readily contribute to their little sister's book until the time when she is old enough to work on it herself.

A memory book is valuable for children at any age. The book grows with them. Their thoughts and feelings as well as their artistic skills are captured on each page. Sally and I talked about the contents of these memory books and how she helped the children work through the loss of their mother during the process. Originally she thought they might like to draw their memories, but the boys decided that they would go through the family pictures instead. The pages are filled with happy moments, letters, decorations. The brothers talked about their mother while busily pasting and writing. They add to the book whenever they want, important events and even not so important events.

Children can have memory books for anyone who is special. Gently suggest the idea to them five or six months after the loss. No two children will respond the same way. Some may want to do it right away, others may want to wait, still others may not want to do it at all. Assist with acquiring the needed materials but remember: let them make the decisions. Suggest they write about the person they miss—that person's appearance, favorite foods, memorable times, fun activities, holidays. Include photographs, memorabilia, and anything else the child mentions. Keep the memory books available, not tucked away on a high self. Look at the book together (you can use the same approach with family albums). This is the kind of book your children will read over and over again. The special moments captured will help your child continue to work through his loss in a very positive way.

Commemoration

An important part of the grieving process is commemorating the life of the person who has died. This allows the memory of the person to live on through the efforts of others. We all need to take part in this process; it is very helpful to us as we come to terms with the loss in our lives. People generally begin to think about commemoration activities several months after their loss. Others, who may not have been as close, may begin to plan activities much sooner. Children find commemoration plans especially important; they view the commemoration as a way of keeping the goals and purposes of the person alive.

After the explosion of the space shuttle *Challenger* in January 1986, thousands of people wrote to the National Aeronautics and Space Administration, the school system of Concord, New Hampshire, and the national Parent-Teacher Association offering suggestions of ways to commemorate the lives of the seven astronauts who had died. In some cases, immediate action was taken, with trust funds for educational purposes and for the advancement of space education established. Toward the end of the first year plans for formal commemoration coalesced. In January 1987 the families of the seven astronauts announced to the public they had decided to set up a living memorial to the crew.

One year ago, we shared a terrible loss with you. The *Challenger* crew ... risked their lives not for the sake of aimless adventure but [for] the nation that gave them opportunity, for the space frontier which was an extension of their spirit. Since their loss we have been troubled by the incompleteness of their mission. Lessons were left untaught ... perhaps saddest of all is the idea that children must once again put their dreams and excitement about the future on hold. This is too great a loss, one we can not accept. We wish to carry on the *Challenger's* mission by creating a network of space learning centers all over the United States, called, cumulatively, the Challenger Center.

—from a "Letter to America" written by the families of the *Challenger* Crew, *New York Times,* January 28, 1987

It takes time to evaluate all the different ways you can commemorate the life of your family member or friend. Children often contribute the most meaningful expressions. We should encourage our children to do something in honor of our friend or relative. Ask them, "What do you think we should do so we always remember Joey?" This encourages children to think about the person who has died in a positive way. What activities did he enjoy? What events were important to him? What were the parts of his life that you would like to remember? How can his life and death be remembered to help others? Answering these questions helps children and their parents come to terms with the senselessness of a death. Through these thoughts and plans we can give meaning and purpose to a person's existence. In future times others will come to know what this person's life meant to those around him.

Some examples of how children have commemorated the life of a person who has died are: scholarship funds through athletic leagues for a child who was active in sports; a tree planted in a family's backyard for their infant daughter; religious articles, such as chalices, in memory of a grandparent; a portrait and the renaming of a school to commemorate the life of the school principal. But efforts need not be as formal as these. Small contributions to funds or organizations, schools, or libraries are equally important. Your children's imagination does not have to be restricted. Encourage them to put their energies into activities that will grow and evolve with time. Encourage them to use their own words and artistic talents. The feelings of gratification will be felt for many months and years to come. When your children think of their loss they will also think of how they helped to keep the memory of that person alive.

Moving Toward the First Anniversary

As the months pass by the first anniversary draws near. Just as we begin to think life is returning to a somewhat normal state there is a strong resurgence of the same old feelings. You ask yourself, "Will I feel this way every year at this time?" The answer is probably yes—but perhaps not with the same intensity as on that first anniversary. The end of the first twelve months of bereavement marks the accomplishment of several important tasks: The most significant part of the grieving process will have taken place, the planning for commemoration and memorial services has been arranged, and family and friends begin to integrate the loss of an important part of their lives into their everyday existence. Children will also notice changes during this time. There is no way to ignore this very emotional event; you have to deal with this just as you have had to cope with all of their other milestones of griefwork.

Help your children be a part of anniversary activities: a visit to the gravesite, dedication of a memorial stone, attendance at a religious service, a gathering of family and friends, or a quiet talk at home with family. It is an important time to stop and reflect on the person who has died and on each individual's work of the past year. There may be a sense of relief once the first year has passed; all of those "firsts" are over. This isn't to say that the second springtime will be any easier. However, the anticipation will be greatly diminished once the special day or time has been experienced for the first time. This first year has probably been one of the most significant in your child's life—a time of tense emotions, family intimacy, and learning. Some families have even commented that they had never felt so close to one other in the months after a relative died. Two fathers admitted to me that they had come to know their children as never before. Circumstances forced them to share parts of their lives with one another. One father continued to say that he found great comfort in sharing his grief with his children. He pointed out that he was not burdening them with his own pain but talking to them in a way that he never had before. Although much pain and sadness accompanies the grieving process, there is also a great deal to be gained. I have used the following fable to help parents and children understand the positive growth that comes from griefwork.

A king once owned a large, beautiful, pure diamond, of which he was justly proud, for it had no equal anywhere. One day, this diamond was accidentally deeply scratched. The king called in the most expert diamond cutters and offered them a great reward if they could remove the imperfection from his jewel. But none could repair the blemish. The king was sorely distressed. After some time a gifted craftsman came to the king and promised to make the rare diamond even more beautiful than it had been before the mishap. The king was impressed by the craftsman's confidence and entrusted to him his precious stone. The man kept his word. With superb artistry he engraved a lovely rosebud around the imperfection, using the scratch to make the stem.
—from I. Klein,
A Time to Be Born,
A Time to Die.
United Synagogue of America, 1977

Death leaves a wound in our beings, much like the scratch in the diamond. When we grieve we are the gifted craftsmen. With time, patience, and encouragement, a rosebud can grow from the deepest scratch.

Sensitive Answers
to Difficult Questions

Your children will ask many of the same questions over and over again throughout the first year of grieving. This doesn't mean that they haven't understood what you have told them; rather, as they grow they are ready for more complicated information. Old answers no longer satisfy their curiosity. For example, a five-year-old may comprehend only that her grandmother's "heart stopped" to cause her death. At ages seven and eight, this same child will understand more about the functioning of the human body and will want to know more of her grandmother's condition. What exactly happened that Grandma's heart stopped? When children are younger we can give simple explanations, and those answers will satisfy them. As they grow older and develop cognitively, simple explanations are no longer sufficient. Be ready to give more information as it is needed. Don't be afraid of overloading your children, but do keep in mind that they won't be ready for all the information you have. Children will feel freer to ask more questions as time passes if you maintain an open mind about their questions. There is nothing more provoking to children than to hear an adult answer their questions with, "You really don't need to know that right now," or "Someday when you're older you'll understand." Give them what they need to know when they ask but gear your answers to their level of understanding.

Michael and Ricky were ten and eight when their aunt died of cancer. She had been taking medication but died several months after her treatment was started. When she died the boys' mother explained to them that the cancer had made their aunt's body very sick. At that time the children asked why the medicine didn't work: When they are sick medicine makes them better; why couldn't it make Aunt Sal better? Two years later one of the boys asked, "But why didn't the medicine work? Why did the cancer keep making her sick and die?" At that point the first explanation was no longer adequate. Michael was ready for more information. At thirteen, interested in his science and health courses, he was able to handle more complex answers. The new information was integrated into the old body of knowledge, satisfying his evolving understanding of his aunt's death.

When your children ask questions that you have already answered, find out what they remember. You then have an awareness of their knowledge base. Build on the information they already have, correct misconceptions, and then proceed to the newer facts. Take your cues from school classes and books. Try to give your new information on the same level as your children's grade level. Even if you're not sure how much to tell your children, don't worry that you may scar them for life because you've told them facts that are above their heads. Ask frequently, "Do you understand?" and give openings for your children to admit that they might not understand what you are talking about.

The following questions and comments are more likely to be asked during the first year. Sometimes children's comments are more difficult than their questions. Responses are provided for you to use or adapt to your own experiences.

Am I ever going to feel better?

"You *will* feel better, but it will take time. I can't give you an exact date that you will begin to feel more like yourself. Gradually, though, you'll notice that you aren't having as many sad feelings and that you are having happier feelings again. It's very hard for you to know exactly when these things will happen, but they will. Even when we feel better, we can still have bad days; this is part of grieving. Sometimes we can still feel sad, but those sad times will happen less and less frequently.

"It takes time to feel better; we can't rush it. There isn't a magical formula to help us feel better faster, but we can talk to other people and share our feelings."

I don't want to have Christmas [or my birthday, etc.] this year. It won't be the same.

"You're right, it won't be the same without Grandma, but not having Christmas won't help us feel any better. We will decide what to do—perhaps we should plan something special to remember Grandma. We can talk about it with the rest of the family. When you begin to feel sad, tell me so we can talk about it together; I might need your help, too."

Avoid saying "Grandma wouldn't want you to do this," or "Grandma would have wanted it this way." In reality, we aren't sure *what* our relative or friend would have wanted. Comments like these make us feel better, but children don't accept such premises. Help your children identify memories of things their relative or friend enjoyed during holiday times. They can then relate to these special events with positive feelings.

I don't want to talk about Grandpa anymore. I just want to forget.

"I know that it makes you feel sad when you talk about Grandpa, but not talking or thinking about him isn't going to make you feel any better. Sometimes people think they can forget. But we don't forget, and it might make it even be harder for us to think about Grandpa.

"If someone starts to talk about Grandpa and you feel sad you might feel like telling that person to be quiet. Instead, I want you to try something else. Ask yourself some questions. What are you feeling when you think of Grandpa? Are you sad? Do you feel angry that he's not here anymore? It takes time to get used to the idea that Grandpa is dead. In the beginning we feel sad every time we think of him, or angry because he's gone, but after a while we will feel happy when we think of Grandpa."

What if I forget about my aunt?

"When people die we think about them a lot. We can't believe that they have died. The more we think about your aunt the more it helps us to know that she really is dead. It becomes real. After a few months we tend not to think about her as much. This doesn't mean that we are forgetting about her. We are getting used to the fact that she is no longer in our daily lives. We don't ever forget about the people we love. We might not think about them every day; instead we think more about them during the more important times, like our birthday or on holidays."

I feel guilty if I begin to have a good time. I think I should still feel sad.

"Grieving doesn't mean that you have to feel sad every minute of every day. It means that we feel sad some of the time. Other times we are happy, especially if we are having a good time or are with people we like. There are times when your mom might feel happy and you'll be sad, and you might even feel angry at her. Everyone is different and grieves in a different way at a different pace."

5

SPECIAL CONSIDERATIONS

Helping Your Children Cope with Violent and Unexpected Deaths

Some circumstances go beyond the normal limits of grieving. These are usually the times complicated by unusual or unexpected situations—suicide, murder or violent death, tragic disaster involving many deaths, or accidents related to alcohol or drug use. In addition to sadness and grief, other emotions complicate our mourning. We can feel anger, frustration, fear, or panic. We tend to deal with these other feelings before we grieve—we put everything else on hold. Sometimes we even lose sight of the fact that a person has died; instead we get caught up in details of crimes, accident reports, and rumors. Children are just as vulnerable to these circumstances. Our children feel what we feel, but more intensely and with less understanding. In an effort to protect them from more pain we may try to keep facts and information hidden. But mystery heightens our children's anxiety and further delays the grieving process. Here are several different situations that may require special consideration as you help your children cope with loss.

Suicide

When people intentionally take their own lives it brings a mixture of reactions from those around them. Sadness is accompanied by anger, as we ask "How could he do that to us?" "Why would she do such a thing?" Inevitably, family members feel guilty. We ask ourselves how we could have prevented the tragedy. We begin our thoughts with "If only . . ." If only we had been at home, if only we had noticed, if only we could have stopped this tragic act. Death by suicide is one of the most difficult losses to grieve for. Griefwork is complicated and prolonged by other feelings. We adults attempt to deal with the shock of suicide by trying to make sense of such a senseless act. Children are confused and angered by the suicide of a family member or friend.

A Suicide in the Family

By nature children, especially young children, tend to be egocentric. So it is not uncommon for children to think that they caused the death of a parent, relative, or friend. As parents, we spend a great deal of time explaining the actual cause of any death to dispel our children's misconceptions. Even when adults have the answers it is a difficult task, but when there are no answers, as in a suicide, our task becomes monumental. Many families try to hide the fact that a person has intentionally taken his or her own life. This never works: children find out sooner or later, usually from someone outside the family. There is absolutely no way to conceal suicide from a child without grave repercussions.

Tom was twenty-five years old and applying to graduate school. While filling out numerous applications he had to answer questions about his parents' health. Tom's mother had died when he was only four years old. Once again he asked his father to explain the cause of his mother's death so he could complete his applications. For some reason Tom's father decided that his son should know the truth about his mother's death at this time. She had committed suicide. Tom's response was one of shock. He felt betrayed. All the old feelings of loss came flooding back to him, but this time he also felt rage—rage and contempt toward his father for keeping this secret from him. Tom did go to graduate school and was quite successful in his career but his relationship with his father has never been the same. It took years before Tom could even talk to his father and stepmother.

Don't compound your children's loss by keeping the whole truth from them. They will need every support available to cope with the legacy of suicide. If we prevent them from knowing that someone in the family has committed suicide we are not helping them effectively grieve for their loss—and we risk alienating them in the future.

How do we tell children about suicide? From the beginning we have to be honest.

"I have something very sad to tell you. Today we learned that your Uncle John died. He took his own life by taking too many pills. We don't know why he did what he did. It is a very sad time for all of us."

We may want to shield our children from learning the method of death but they will find out anyway. You needn't give every detail but do be factual. The less information we give our children the more fantasy they will create, and that will frighten them more than the truth.

The sense of shock and disbelief make the early hours following a suicide very difficult, as people are afraid to verbalize their thoughts. Include all family members, especially brothers and sisters, when sharing feelings regarding a suicide. Children often push ideas out of their heads as too bizarre or too scary. An environment of closeness and love will provide a sense of security to them. When adults verbalize their thoughts, they allow children to talk about their own feelings.

The question of "why?" is foremost in our minds. Siblings will also want the answer to that difficult question. Be honest; if you know the underlying reason for the suicide, don't hide it. Give your children an opportunity to explore and understand on their own.

Many children, especially teenagers, fantasize that they will somehow find themselves in the same situation without warning. Reassure children that people *do* give warning signs, although they may be hard to see. Siblings may fear that the same fate will befall them. Talking about one's concerns and fears is an important way to avoid such tragedy. Reassure your children of your support and love for them. Ask them to help you be a better listener; let them know that no concern is too trivial. This information is very comforting to a child who is terrified of an unseen force within their psyche.

Every parent who has lost a child or a friend's child to suicide may fear that other children in the family will repeat the act. Dwelling on that fear—saying, for example, "I hope you never do this to me"—will not provide a feeling of security to your children. They may have the same frightening thoughts. You do not want to cause a child who is desperate to shy away, fearing that he will be disappointing you.

Acknowledge the confusion and feelings people have when someone they love commits suicide. This helps your children feel they are not alone or unusual. We all need support when we lose a family member or friend, and it seems we need more if death has been intentional. Children, like adults, have to face friends and relatives who know or suspect what has happened. Do not tell your children to avoid talking about the death to others. Painful though it is, we cannot keep friends, neighbors, or even the community from knowing the truth.

Suicide has stigma and shame attached to it in our society. We tend to cover it up rather then deal with it, grieving for a suicide victim in secret. If people are hesitant to talk to us when we've experienced a loss, they avoid us at all costs when there is a suicide in the family. For these reasons we must maintain open communication with our children at all times. By encouraging our children to talk about their feelings with us, we let them know that we are willing to share this burden with them.

A Suicide in School

These days, we hear about adolescent suicide everywhere—newspapers, magazines, television. It is a concern on everyone's mind. We're not sure if there really is a drastic increase or if we just hear about it more because people are more open to revealing the truth. A suicide in a school sends shock waves through the entire student body, teachers, and all parents in the community. Honesty with your children is the best approach. If you don't know what has happened, admit that to your children. Try to give them as much factual information as possible. There will be enough rumors and distorted information as it is.

Your challenge will be to help your children grieve. Children and adolescents in particular will be frightened. Their curiosity and fear can prevent them from identifying feelings of loss and grief. Teenagers may portray a "cool" side to their peers, not wanting to admit how much they are upset by a death in the school community. Recently I worked with some students following a suicide in the school. While most reacted with sadness and concern, several students said, "Well, he was a druggie anyway," or "No one really knew him, he kept to himself." With thoughts like these we keep at a distance. We do not have to be as emotionally involved—we don't have to grieve, or so we think. In fact, when we do this we try to deny that the loss has an effect on us, something teenagers frequently try to do. If you hear your children or teenagers saying something to this effect, you can intervene, saying, "Well, it still must be hard to accept the fact that someone your age has taken his own life. I know it scares me."

The truth *is* very frightening: someone who is very much like your own children—the same age, maybe the same sex, possibly similar interests—has taken his own life. What made this child take such drastic measures? How can you be sure that your children or one of their friends won't feel the same way? We sometimes fear—maybe irrationally, maybe not—that suicide is contagious. That feeling may be at the root of our need to keep suicides secret. But when we keep information from our children we make the event more dramatic and intriguing than ever.

Adolescents may also feel a sense of guilt. Perhaps they could have prevented their classmate's death in some way. In some cases, teenagers may actually hear or talk to a classmate who is threatening suicide. Thinking that their friend is being dramatic or joking, they dismiss the comments only to find out later that the threat was serious. If this has happened to your children they may feel very much responsible for their friend's death. They will need a great deal of support and possibly professional counseling to put the events in perspective.

As parents and concerned teachers we need to support young people at times like this. Allow them to talk about their feelings inside the classroom as well as in small groups. You may find that they are reluctant to share their feelings because the situation is so terrifying for them. They identify very closely with their peers. They ask the question, "If my friend did this because she was depressed or broke up with her boyfriend or got bad grades, would I do the same thing?" With children at any age we must make sure they know that there are more ways to solve problems than suicide, that there are other options and there will always be someone to talk to.

Violent Death

Children frequently hear about violence in our communities and in our entire society. When the violence touches their own homes and neighborhoods it presents a much greater problem than those events related by the media. A murder in the community strikes terror in the hearts of every family. Grief is overshadowed by fear. Rumors abound throughout the town. Parents and families take protective measures to ensure the safety of their children.

In a small suburban community in the Northeast an eleven-year-old girl was murdered on her way home from school. She was strangled to death and her body was left in the woods. Distraught school administrators faced the task of informing the students and parents. They decided to announce the facts of the death to all students. The children were shocked and frightened, but they did ask questions; they did want to know what had happened. When the parents learned of the news from their sons and daughters they feared for the safety of their children but they were also angry. Many felt that the parents in the community should have been told first, or should have been able to inform the children themselves.

There is shock and panic everywhere in the early hours of a community crisis such as this. It is difficult to know exactly the right course of action. Many parents felt they did not want their children to hear the details surrounding the death of this young girl, but school officials wanted students to have accurate information to decrease the rumors and misconceptions of the children. For weeks parents would not allow their children to go anywhere alone. They drove them to school, didn't let them out after dark, and escorted them to community functions. There was an air of fear and concern throughout the town. Each time new facts were revealed from the investigation the terror was recharged.

In cases of violent death we must help our children separate the fear of the crime from the sadness of the loss. When we focus on fear, on safety, and on the criminal aspects of the situation, we dwell on the crime that has been committed rather than the life that has been lost. We don't allow our children to grieve for their peer.

It is difficult to deal with the feelings surrounding violent death. We must acknowledge safety but we also need to mourn the loss of a classmate and friend.

Griefwork may be prolonged or put on hold while other aspects of the death gain attention. As fear is resolved griefwork intensifies. Children are still mourning years later. At such times, we must think about how we can truly help our children. We can teach them caution and safety, but they really need us to help them cope with the death.

Our immediate reaction to families of those who have lost a member through a violent death is to stay away, hoping irrationally that we will protect ourselves from danger. The sensational nature of the death keeps us separate from the people who need us the most—good friends, neighbors, and even siblings. Remind yourself that these people are important to you and that they need you, especially the children. Ostracism will only complicate griefwork. Anger and resentment will further alienate families, friends, and neighbors. For these situations long-term support is especially important. Be there for the family after the funeral and first weeks of mourning. Continued caring and concern will help people get through the difficult months ahead, when investigations and trials reactivate intense feelings of grief.

Accidents

Nothing hurts us more than death that is both senseless and preventable. While many circumstances fit this category, automobile accidents related to alcohol and drug use seem to sting the most. Often the victims are young—teenagers celebrating prom night or graduation, college students away from home and experimenting with newfound freedom. Such accidents involve two kinds of victims: the person who dies because of someone else's actions and the person who dies as a result of his own actions. Survivors are left with a confusing array of emotions—shock, sadness, and anger, often directed toward the victim as well as the person responsible for the accident.

In the early hours following an accident, facts are sketchy, initial reactions clouded and confused. People may not be sure who is the victim and who is responsible. Our feelings of frustration and helplessness lead us to begin every sentence with the words, "If only . . ." As parents we sometimes fall into the "I told you so . . ." lectures. We caution our children about crossing the street, buckling their seat belts, roughhousing with each other. Suddenly, our dire predictions come true. We need to be more careful not to add to our children's anxiety or even guilt following a tragic accident. I've heard many children and adolescents say, "Don't punish me because of what happened to someone else!" We tend to tighten the reins, hoping to protect our own children from danger, but by focusing on the safety and prevention we lose sight of the need to grieve.

Anger, always a part of the griefwork process, will surface—months, perhaps years, later. Anger is a normal emotion when someone has died. We try to find someone to blame for the tragedy. When death is accidental it is easier to focus our feelings on someone else; the driver of the car, the friend who extended the party invitation, even the person who has died. Anger can become irrational, and it may seem that no amount of talking can diminish that anger. It takes time to move through this period. Sometimes people use their anger and other emotions in productive ways, introducing new laws, petitions, support groups, activist groups, even writing. All of these activities are helpful and allow people to express their feelings in socially acceptable ways.

Children can be helped in much the same way. We

can encourage them to identify their feelings, then act on them. For young children drawing or telling stories is helpful. Older children may also draw, write stories or poetry, or become involved in community groups. Teenagers can become involved in many of the same activities as parents and teachers. But children have to feel comfortable with their own ways of expressing their feelings; not everyone can put aside raw emotions for productive activities. Consider talking to a professional if a child's anger—or your own—becomes destructive to the child or others, or if the anger lasts for much longer than you expected.

As far as emotions go, there is no right or wrong, no good or bad. I know of one father who still holds onto his rage toward the family of the boy who was driving the car the night his son was killed. On the other hand, there are people who seem to have endless compassion for the family and person responsible for the death of a loved one.

At one Midwestern university a student was driving while drunk and killed another student who was walking on campus. The father of the dead child actually went to meet the family of the driver, embraced the father, and said, "I know my son will be all right where he is; we have to help your son through this terrible ordeal."

Not everyone can say those words. Eventually, even the angriest people will be able to feel a sense of compassion and the most compassionate will slowly get in touch with their anger. Help your children see the spectrum of emotions without labeling them "good" or "bad." By allowing them to experience their feelings without censure we keep the door open and encourage future communication.

When Death Comes Instead of Birth: Miscarriage, Stillbirth, Sudden Infant Death Syndrome

Accidental death surprises and shocks us because it is unanticipated. When death comes in place of the joyous birth of a new baby, our grief must replace the elation we had expected. We anticipate joy and instead experience loss; we look forward to a new human being and indeed must mourn a person we never knew. All of the hopes and dreams we imagined for this new person are shattered, never to come to life. This is the case when there is a stillbirth, miscarriage, or sudden death of an infant.

Grieving an infant is difficult. Well-meaning friends and relatives often supply words that are intended to offer comfort and support but fall short: "You're young, you can have more children." For too long our society has overlooked the loss of an infant or a pregnancy. We must grieve for these tiny individuals just as we mourn the loss of those we have known for many years. We need to help our children comprehend what has happened in their family.

Because siblings are usually younger children and have limited understanding of pregnancy and birth, their questions are difficult to answer. Be as direct as you possibly can and use words that are understandable. If possible let the children talk or see their mother as soon as convenient. You need to let them know that their mother is all right; separation anxiety can be intensified with fantasies of mother loss. There will be many questions and comments as they try to integrate the experience. Answer those questions with patience.

If the infant has been at home your children will have memories of the baby, its appearance and behavior. A miscarriage is different, for your child cannot remember a baby they never saw or knew. Instead, focus on feelings: sadness, disappointment, and unmet expectations. If there has been a stillbirth you can do several things to help your child come to know the baby. If you want to and if the baby has not been injured or grossly deformed, you may consider taking a photograph of the baby's face and showing it to your children. You can also describe the infant to them: the weight, length, hair color, and other identifiable family characteristics. Some families have even shown the infant to older children for a few minutes. These suggestions are important for you as well as your children.

Sibling rivalry begins long before the birth of a new brother or sister. Even the most enthusiastic older sibling looks upon the new arrival as an interference. Children have fantasies of "getting rid" of this new interloper. If this expected baby dies some children will somehow interpret the loss as their fault; at the least they will have guilt feelings for their unkind thoughts. Reassure your children that they had nothing to do with the loss of the baby. Explain to them, according to their level of understanding, the reason for the baby's death. Try not to say, "This baby was so special that God wanted him." Young children will interpret this explanation to mean that they were not special, reinforcing the idea that they somehow did something wrong.

Include your children in any funeral or memorial services. It is not easy for anyone to look at a casket only three feet long, but it is important for the entire family to be a part of this experience. Don't minimize the impact this loss has on your children—it is a significant loss and one they will not forget.

Twenty-seven-year old Tim shared his memories of his stillborn sister when his wife was pregnant. He feared for their own unborn child and talked about the feelings he had had at age eleven. "I remember my father coming home from the hospital. He looked sad and I knew something was wrong. He told us the baby had died. All I could think about was how much we all looked forward to this baby: the little clothes in the drawers, the crib in the new room, and the names we picked out. I think her name was Sarah. I never knew what she looked like and I don't remember talking about her. We didn't want to make my mother feel sadder."

Future pregnancies in the family may precipitate more questions and fears from children. This is to be expected. Be hopeful and tell your children that most babies are born healthy, just like they were, but that things go wrong sometimes and the baby doesn't develop properly and dies because it can't live outside of the mother's body. Let your children talk about their feelings. They may be better able to express them later on than immediately after the baby has died. Grief can be a lonely experience, but if we share it with our children we are helping ourselves as well as the younger members of our family.

The Suddenness of Death

In all of these situations death catches us by surprise. We are not prepared and don't expect a person to be taken away from us. What begins as a normal day in the morning collapses into a surrealistic nightmare within a matter of hours. We cannot prepare. We cannot anticipate. We are raw and exposed to the most painful experience we will ever have. Because of this vulnerability we may have more griefwork to do than if we had expected the death.

News of a sudden death evokes feelings of shock, disbelief, panic, and disorganization. It takes time to comprehend what has happened. We feel as though we are going crazy. During the first hours and days we need people to help give us direction, to tell us when to eat and sleep, to help us make decisions about arrangements. Children have the same feelings, but they also witness the behavior of their parents. Their feelings of helplessness are magnified by the fact that the single most stabilizing force in their lives is no longer able to provide a sense of security.

Although you want to give them the sense of security they need, don't try to hide your own feelings and behavior from your children. They need to see you even if you're not in the best shape. If possible, tell them these feelings won't last, that you—and they—will be all right again. If you are unable to speak to your children, have someone else help. Physical contact is very important at this time. Even if you are unable to talk to your children, give them a hug, tuck them in bed at night, hold them on your lap. They will feel less frightened for their own security if you can give them familiar signs.

After any death, especially a sudden death, we are preoccupied with thoughts of the person who has died. In addition, we ask, "Why did this have to happen to me?" Sometimes there are no answers. We go over the details of the day's events, always looking for a different ending or an explanation. Your children will ask the same questions and talk about the same thoughts. Tell them you have the same feelings yourself. This confirms that they are not alone or unusual. Most of all, it encourages them to continue to share with you.

Sensitive Answers
to Difficult Questions

These may be some of the most difficult questions you will have to answer, in part because you may not have the answers yourself. Try to be as honest as you can. Be sure you *know* the facts first before you give your child any information. Be as honest as you can. Questions regarding violent deaths or very special circumstances not only deal with grief and loss but also with safety, coping, relationships, and unexpected outcomes.

Why did he do it?

"I'm not sure why your uncle took his own life. Sometimes people are so sad that they think no one else can help. They think the only way to get rid of their troubles is to die. That's not true; there are lots of ways to get help, and there will always be someone who cares about you and will listen to your problems.

"Your uncle couldn't tell us he needed help, and we didn't see how sad he was. It makes us all feel very sad—sad because we love him and miss him, and sad because we didn't know he needed our help."

He was a jerk, anyway. It's no big deal!

"You may not have liked Sam very much but his death must still hurt. When someone close to our own age and grade decides that he can no longer live, it makes us think about ourselves. It's scary.

You begin to wonder if you might do the same thing, or maybe one of your friends—someone you really care about. Even if Sam wasn't your favorite person his death makes you think about living and dying; it makes all of us think about it. Whatever was on Sam's mind, he must have felt terribly alone, so alone that he couldn't ask anyone to help him. No one should ever feel that alone. Suicide is not a way to solve your problems. There will always be someone who loves you enough to talk to you and help you solve your problems. No problem is more important than life itself."

Will you [or I] do the same thing?

"I know this must be something you think about. Since your dad died you must think that one of us might do the same thing. His death has made all of us think about how much we love each other and care about the other people in our family. Talking to each other is the best way we can prevent feeling alone. I care about you and your brothers. Suicide is *not* the only option for solving our problems. We can always work something out no matter how bad you think things are. I worry about all of you thinking that the way Dad tried to solve his problems was good. It wasn't—but we still can't help having those feelings."

I was bad—that's why she killed herself!

"You did not cause your mom to die. She had feelings about herself that none of us could understand. She was very sad, and she thought that she

was doing the right thing by dying. We can't understand why she felt that way. What happened to
Mom had nothing to do with you; it had to do with
the thoughts she had in her own mind."

This needs to be reinforced over and over again, especially with younger children.

I'm afraid I'll get killed too!

"When there is a murder we are scared. We try to
be more careful and stay safe. We should always be
careful about where we go and what we do, but we
can't stay locked in the house forever. Remember,
these kinds of things don't happen very often. Also,
the police are very careful about finding the person
who did this and making sure he is kept away from
others so it won't happen again."

Why did he have to drink and drive?

"I don't know the answer. Maybe Bobby thought
he was able to handle drinking and still be a safe
driver. But no one can drink and be a safe driver,
no matter how old they are. You must feel angry
that Bobby did not use good judgment. We sometimes feel angry at the person who has died. That's
normal. We want to blame someone for what has
happened. We feel helpless that we couldn't stop
him from dying. And we will all miss him very
much."

But why did the baby die?

"The doctors at the hospital told us that your brother had a problem with his ———. (Give a simple explanation of the cause of death.) He couldn't live on his own and there was no way to help him. We don't know why some babies are born with problems and others, like you, are not. Most babies are born healthy. But we still wonder why it happened to our baby."

Well, they can always have another baby!

"That's true, they *can* have another baby. But that doesn't mean that we should forget about this baby. He was going to be a part of the family just like the other children. It doesn't help us to push away our feelings. Aunt Jane and Uncle Jim feel sad, and we can't hurry them through their feelings or try to make them feel better by talking about other babies. When the time comes for them to have another baby, they will be happy, but they'll always remember this baby."

6

LOOKING TOWARD THE FUTURE

Griefwork and Important Events in the Years Ahead

After the first year, you and your children begin to adjust to the absence of the person who has died. Although memories are still strong, family and friends move on with their lives, making the necessary changes. We all encounter situations that bring back the pain of loss, and sometimes the pain seems as intense as it was the day of the funeral. The words are all too familiar: "Your father would have loved to see you on this day." "Your mother would have been so proud." For children, these significant events span the rest of their lives—graduating from school, learning how to drive, and going away to camp are a few examples. We need to prepare our children for these bittersweet times when joy and sadness mix together. Our children will grow because of these events, but we need to give them tools for cultivating that growth.

Changes and Losses Throughout Life

Children have to cope with their early losses during significant turning points later in their lives. These turning points are often called milestones in human development—entering a new school, graduating from high school, getting married, moving, and having a child. These events involve change and can have a negative or positive influence on our behavior. We adults have already experienced many of these milestones; our children have many of these experiences to anticipate.

We all carry emotional baggage—echoes of past events that influence the present and the future. Children have to carry their baggage for a longer distance than adults so it is important to pack the contents with care from the beginning. During those early days and weeks of griefwork children are "packing" their emotional suitcases. Unconsciously they weigh each thought and feeling before putting it away.

Some children don't want to look at what they have to carry. They cram all their emotions into the suitcase and try to shut it as soon as possible. If they're not careful, though, feelings hang out, caught between the sides. These children may appear to have coped, but soon we see those caught emotions: anger, aggression, frustration, and loneliness. Other children succeed in shutting all of their thoughts and feelings in the bag. They push the top down and force those emotions to stay inside. Eventually, however, they will have to reopen that suitcase, maybe at another time of loss, maybe at an important turning point in their lives. When they do open it, the suitcase explodes, and all of those feelings will tumble out. Sometimes the suitcase will spring open even when its owner wants to keep it shut. These are the times when children least expect to deal with their grief. Sometimes children attempt to lock the suitcase, never trying to talk about or allow themselves to feel their grief, ever again. Their burden becomes heavier as they grow older, and, as a result, these children have difficulty with all emotional aspects of their lives.

As parents, we certainly cannot pack our children's bags for them, but we can be there to supervise and give support. We can see that our children load their feelings and thoughts so they can be carried comfortably. We can help our children know the nature of their burden for knowing the contents of the suitcase makes the load easier to carry. We can tell our children that there will be other times in their lives when these feelings will have to be unpacked, unfolded, and put away again, especially at significant milestones.

How many times have you yourself remembered a favorite deceased relative at one of those important times in your own life? When children have early, significant losses they must do more than have passing thoughts. They need to regrieve their loss in light of the new experience in their lives.

Diana was twenty-three and planning to be married. The wedding was quickly approaching, with the usual busy preparations. Diana found herself thinking of her grandmother who had died seven years earlier; "How she would have enjoyed this!" She also felt pangs of loneliness and sadness. Diana wanted to do something special in her grandmother's memory. She decided to leave her wedding bouquet on her grandmother's grave. She also had a smaller bouquet made to use for the traditional toss of the bouquet at the reception. Since the cemetery was some distance away from the reception, Diana's parents placed the bouquet on the grave the next day. They even took a photograph of the beautiful cream-colored roses and silken ribbons gently floating in the breeze in front of the memorial stone.

Diana's plan included the whole family and enabled her to continue to work through her feelings of grief. She "rearranged" the contents of her "suitcase" at an important time in her life. Seventeen years later she still thinks of that day and the gesture of remembrance to her grandmother.

When we open that suitcase and rearrange the contents we think of the loss in our lives and what it means to us. We also think of the life event at hand and try to integrate the two together. If we don't regrieve those early losses our burden of grief becomes heavier and heavier. Then, when we least expect it and are least prepared for it, our emotions pour out in a flood. Sometimes, unresolved grief can even affect our emotional functioning in other areas of our lives.

> Jean was a graduate student in psychology. She had been working with a client for several months in therapy. During one of their weekly sessions he began to recount the death of his grandfather when he was a child. Jean listened and helped him identify his feelings of loss. As usual, she transcribed her taped session onto paper for her supervisor to review. She recalled feeling a bit uncomfortable as she heard her client on the tape talking about his grandfather's death. Later she had to read her session in front of her professor and peers. When she started to talk about the death of the grandfather, words would not come out of her mouth. Tears filled her eyes and she broke down in sobs. Jean finally shared with the group that she was reminded of her own grandfather's death when she was very young. Jean's professor quietly suggested that she probably had more grieving to do for her own grandparent. For the first time Jean was able to express just how much she missed her grandfather.

There are other occasions when children need to regrieve early losses. Every time we have a loss in our lives, old feelings are stirred up from earlier experiences. After the *Challenger* exploded in 1986 I had a discussion with some third graders. I asked them to talk about their feelings. They told me that they felt sad, they cried, got angry, and felt bad. I then asked if this was like any other time in their lives. Immediately hands were raised. "When my grandfather died." "When my dog was killed." "When my bird flew away."

Old losses, resurfacing again—and needing to be dealt with again. This is true not only for children but for adults as well.

Children cannot pass through one of life's momentous occasions or significant losses without thinking of earlier times. These thoughts bring sadness and even intense feelings of loneliness. Each time a child faces a normal milestone he must reopen his suitcase and grieve the loss again. This is one of the most important differences between adult and childhood griefwork: Adults have been through many of those milestones; children have not.

Use the analogy of the loaded suitcase to help your children understand the work that is ahead of them. Let them know that the packing they do now will help them later in their lives. Assure your children that you will help them and share this job with them. If they think the suitcase is becoming heavy, you can open it together. You both can look at those thoughts and feelings, sharing them with each other. Help your children stay in touch with their feelings. Your encouragement will give them the preparation they need for the times when you are not around.

Hearts and Unicorns

Somewhere toward the end of the first year and into the second year of bereavement we begin to integrate the loss of a special person into our daily lives. We get used to the absence and at the same time strengthen our memories of the qualities we loved so much. A mother called me one evening and told me that she had realized something very important about the meaning of her son's life. She had found a symbol of his existence—this symbol was neither depressing nor shrinelike, but rather an uplifting phenomenon that wove throughout her daily life.

Jimmy was a robust and energetic eleven-year-old when he died quite suddenly. He was an avid player of Dungeons and Dragons. He enjoyed the mythical entities of Old English folklore, especially the unicorn. Jimmy's mother found that the family had come to use a unicorn as a symbol of his life. On the piano in the family room was a collection of unicorns. They were placed next to the wrestling trophies and medals belonging to Jimmy's brothers.

With such a symbol we continue to validate the importance of the person who has died. The symbol is truly a daily reminder or special way we have of remembering the person who has died. A part of that person lives on every day with us. Fond memories and warm feelings replace the ache of those early months. This isn't to say that sad feelings do not return periodically—they do. The symbol is a sign of growth, a way for us to know that we're going to be okay, that we will laugh again, enjoy life again, and still not forget the person who has died. It is meaningful not only in its direct reflection of the interests of that person but also because of the relationship shared with others. When we lose someone close to us we lose the special parts of that relationship. Perhaps we bantered or joked, argued and debated, or just shared good books. Symbols remind us that even though we cannot replace the person we can look for those qualities important to us in our relationships with others.

Katie was two years old when she died after cardiac surgery. She was a special child because she also had Down's syndrome. Katie's death caused great pain to all who knew her, but her existence has come to symbolize more than anyone could imagine. People were united in their grief. A special bond developed among friends who shared the loss with Katie's mother, Susan. Monthly support groups evolved into sessions where everyone shared their feelings of loss and separation. There was a real sense of reaching out. Several months later Susan began to sign letters with a small heart drawn below her name. Everyone knew what it meant. Love and caring had evolved from the tragedy of a child's death. People who know Susan and the rest of the family cannot help but think of the goodness Katie brought to those around her, symbolized by a heart.

Symbols grow from the griefwork we must do to resolve our loss. We find symbols when we let ourselves think of fond memories of the person who has died— their favorite things, their hobbies, their special interests, and most of all what we loved best about them. A symbol can't be forced; it arises spontaneously and seems to grow more valid with time.

I have found that parents and children who openly

talk about their loss and the meaning of a symbol have grown from the pain in their lives. The search for a symbol is something that your children can truly appreciate. It becomes a concrete way for them to remember someone close to them. The memories and feelings attached to our chosen symbols, our "hearts and unicorns" are very private; they are far stronger and last longer than photographs or words.

Finding the Meaning of Loss

When we are grappling with the pain of loss we find it hard to find the good in such a terrible experience. But there *is* good, and there *can* be growth. I have tried to find ways to explain this perplexing phenomenon to young people by using analogies. This is the one I like best. I would like to share it with you so you can share it with your children.

Grief is like a butterfly. Before the butterfly is ready to go free in the world it has to go through changes. While all these changes are taking place the caterpillar is very vulnerable and must stay safe in a cocoon. When we are grieving, we are much the same. When someone we love dies it hurts us. Sometimes the only way we can feel better is to stay in our own little cocoon. We stay in that cocoon for a while, experiencing different thoughts and feelings about the person who has died. That is what grieving is all about: having those thoughts and feelings, sharing them with other people, and protecting ourselves a little bit, as if we were in a safe cocoon. As time goes by we don't need that protective cocoon as much. We want to spread our wings . . .

7

GETTING HELP

Deciding When and Who to Ask For Help

When we are faced with a crisis we tend to use skills that we never knew we had. We rise to the occasion and deal with the situation as best we can. Death is probably the most difficult crisis we will have to face in our lives. Loss renders us helpless. We lose control. We cannot make the situation better by bringing back our family member. When our children experience a loss we grieve for their pain as well as our own. Many of the things we do and say to help children work through their grief are helpful for us to remember as we try to manage crises. Child or adult, we need to:

• Recognize and admit what has happened.

• Include our families in what is happening and share the feelings surrounding the event.

• Accept the help and support of others, knowing that they would want our friendship and caring during their time of need.

• Try to be flexible about demands on ourselves. Difficult times call for modifying our standards.

• Break problems down into small manageable parts and take each step as it comes.

• Try to express our own feelings in a caring, nonburdening way.

- Avoid making hasty decisions or major life changes too soon. We and our children need the stability of the familiar in times of crisis.

- Remember that the passage of time will help everyone get used to new roles and situations.

- Try to remain hopeful and patient. Working our way out of crisis, and grieving in particular, takes time.

- Consider seeking professional help if our own efforts seem inadequate after a reasonable amount of time.

What is a reasonable length of time? How do we know when we—or our children—need professional help? How do we know when our children are coping well with the death of a friend or family member? All children react to loss in an individual way. Much depends on their personalities and previous experiences. You will know which behaviors are alien to your children.

Give both yourself and your children an adequate period of time to resolve the loss. That time might be a year or more. Review the points in Chapter 4 describing behavior and depression in children. If others are telling you that they are concerned about your children's behavior, listen to them! Sometimes we as parents cannot see what is obvious to teachers and friends. It cannot harm your children to talk to someone who is knowledgeable about children and griefwork. You might even consider seeing a counselor for a short time—six weeks or so—to help you focus on your children's needs and possibly your own as well.

There are special situations in which it might be a good idea to meet with a counselor early on.

- If your children have had any previous emotional counseling, you may want to talk with the counselor again. This is not to say your children will have problems grieving a loss because of past difficulties.

Rather, sometimes approaches that were successful in the past can be useful in a new crisis.

- When very young children suffer a loss, particularly of a parent, they may need special help to assist them in verbalizing their feelings. Sometimes this is best accomplished through the services of a child therapist, one who uses play therapy techniques.

- Children with development disabilities need as much guidance and support as other children. You can use any of the suggestions I've mentioned in this book, applying them according to your children's cognitive age. Share your children's loss with others who may be involved in their care and education—teachers, counselors, workshop managers, or house managers. Emotional maturity is not always consistent with cognitive level—a child on a third-grade cognitive level may have less mature emotional response when dealing with a loss.

If, after a reasonable period of time, you feel that things are not going well, it is time to talk to someone. Friends try to help as much as they can, sometimes getting in over their heads. People who care about us usually find it difficult to tell us they can no longer help with our problems. Listen for cues. If you find yourself talking to the same person each morning for an hour it might be time to find a counselor. Friends and relatives can provide a great support but when your friends seem to be frustrated or too busy to listen, then it is time to talk to someone professionally. If you have ever worked with a counselor and found the experience helpful, consider contacting this person again. If you don't know where to begin, there are several guidelines to help you make your choice. A trusted health professional may be able to give you several recommendations. You might even know a friend or colleague who could give you several referrals. Some people prefer to work with a professional with a religious orientation. Ask your clergyman who he might suggest; perhaps he may be willing to see you himself. Listings in public telephone directories don't provide enough information about mental health professionals. However, if this is your only option, look for professionals who are certified and licensed in their field. Community mental health centers and service organizations offer counseling as well, but you may have to wait to be seen by a professional. You have many choices in the field of mental health: physicians, psychiatric nurses, social workers, and psychologists. One is not better than the other. However, it is important to find someone you feel comfortable with.

How do you know who that person is? After you have identified at least three mental health professionals, call each one and explain what your needs are. Talk with them about their approach, fees, office hours, and whether or not they have done bereavement counseling before. If you like, make an appointment to see each one and make your decision on that basis. Give yourself a chance to work with this new person. Often relief isn't apparent on the first visit. Give yourself at least six sessions. This gives you time to get to know the counselor and vice versa. Friends may want to help and give you advice on who you should see or when you should stop counseling. This is a decision best worked out between you and your counselor. You know your situation better than anyone else. Even with help, you may feel as if you are going crazy. This is normal. As one father told me, "The best advice I ever got was to *expect* to feel crazy, that the world would be upside down ... Once I knew I wasn't really 'losing it,' I just tried to ride out the next months." This man also told me that he found reassurance in talking with others in similar situations.

We can learn from each other. You may even consider attending—or organizing—community support groups for parents or children. Reach out to others, and let people reach out to you. If this advice sounds like what I've told you to do with your children, it is. Sometimes we need to be pushed to follow our own advice.

8

FOR TEACHERS, CLERGY, AND OTHER CONCERNED ADULTS

8:15 in the morning, the day after Joey died. The school bus slows at the familiar stop but no one enters the bus. The seat next to the window remains empty. Not one child's voice can be heard. This morning there is no laughter or teasing. The ride takes twenty minutes but it seems like an eternity. The fifth graders file out of the bus and into their classroom. Another sign of the sadness is soon apparent: Joey's desk is empty. The children walk quietly around the room as if this piece of classroom equipment is a shrine.

There had been much discussion since the fatal accident had occurred the evening before. Parents, teachers, and school administrators tried to decide the best way to handle the crisis. But no decisions were made; instead everyone agreed to try their best. But "trying one's best" can not possibly prepare the teacher or her students for what will happen in the hours and days ahead.

When a child, teacher, or parent dies there is a ripple effect within the community. At first glance it appears that only those who are immediately associated with the family need support, but a closer look tells us that others are involved.

Daniel's younger brother Michael was in the first grade when he was diagnosed with acute leukemia.

The disease never went into remission, and Michael was absent for most of the first three months of the school year. After ten months of unsuccessful treatment Michael died during the summer. The loss was felt by his first-grade classmates and, of course, his teachers. But there were others not as close yet just as involved, who felt the effects: classmates of Michael's sixth-grade brother and his third-grade sister, and their families, as well.

Michael's death was felt by adults and children alike in the school and in the community: classmates, teachers, Cub Scout leaders, and parents of other children. Every person touched by the loss needed support. The question remains, though: How can we help? So often we are afraid to get involved or fear we will say the wrong thing. The following sections will provide guidance for those who are not members of the immediate family but who feel the pain of loss indirectly.

Teachers: The First Line of Defense

I strongly believe our children's teachers are their strongest support and their best line of defense. Teachers see children every day in a consistent and structured environment. Often students will say or do things in school that they would not do at home. The teacher's involvement can be a significant influence on children's grieving.

One Friday evening in the spring a group of high school students went out for coffee and donuts following a baseball game. There had been drinking earlier in the evening and "inexperience behind the wheel." When a police car attempted to stop the teenagers, the driver impulsively tried to outrun the patrol car. Within minutes the students' car crashed into a telephone pole, killing Jim, a passenger in the front seat. The other five were not injured. The following Monday none of the accident victims were in school although the story was circulated throughout the student body. Friends of the six students were upset by the reactions of the people in their school. One boy was shocked to see that his first-period teacher removed Jim's chair and went on with business as usual. "Not one mention of my friend; she didn't even say she was sorry he died!" Another student noticed that her teacher was very uncomfortable and couldn't talk about the situation. "She was more upset than we were!" Other classmates reported that their teachers made time to talk whenever they needed.

There is no one, sure-fire way to deal with students who feel vulnerable after the loss of a classmate or friend, but you can be sure that "no effort" will turn off your class quickly—whether they are in first grade or eleventh grade!

Talking in Groups

Group discussion is critical when working with students in these circumstances. For preschool and primary grade children the discussions should be brief and structured. It is best if the group meeting takes place in familiar surroundings with familiar people. Young children take comfort in hearing the comments and questions of their peers. Often the discussion becomes tangential and requires refocusing. Afterwards you can ask the children to draw pictures. Their artwork will serve as a springboard for further talks and can provide some useful insight into the children's perceptions of loss. You can also ask the children to draw cards or pictures. In many cases the class will spontaneously decide to send the pictures or stories to the grieving family. In doing so, children are working through their own feelings and also reaching out to others. If a fellow classmate has died, you may have to repeat your talks and opportunities for picture drawing weeks after the death. Remember this "talking time" cannot be planned. If you hear children talking about death or the dead person, encourage them to share their thoughts with you and their classmates.

Different Ages, Different Approaches

Elementary school children tend to accept the irreversibility of death, but they are curious about the facts of death, life after death, and bodies after death. Group discussions are of great importance at this age. As these students begin to focus on their own grief reactions, emphasize that their feelings are normal. Ask your students to talk about other times in their lives when they may have had similar feelings, what they do to feel better when they have sad thoughts, and what they can do to remember the dead.

Participation in memorial services and funeral practices can be appropriate for this age group. Children feel important and useful if they can show how much they cared for the person who has died. Your role as a teacher can include facilitating students' participation: arranging transportation, writing letters or poetry, or sending flowers or contributions. Be sure to work closely with parents; they are experiencing the same reactions as you and your students.

Joey was to be buried the day before Thanksgiving. The principal of Joey's school decided that the students needed more time to get to the funeral services, so he dismissed school an hour earlier. Children, teachers, and staff filed into the church anxiously. After the minister spoke, four of Joey's closest friends read aloud to the congregation, talking about their feelings for their friend, what was special about him, what they liked, and what they would miss the most. It was not an easy time for the teachers and parents, but fellow students listened with genuine understanding.

As children enter adolescence they have a much more sophisticated understanding of death. Yet their emotionality and struggle for a new identity often complicate the grieving process. An adolescent perceives himself as invincible, a sort of immortal hero in a teen fairy tale. Fear and disbelief envelop the adolescent as he is confronted with his own mortality. Group discussions with teenagers are often directed toward the issues of identity and feelings centered around the "unfairness" of life. Some students who have difficulty sharing their feelings in front of their peers may need additional time with a teacher, school nurse, or counselor.

Special Circumstances

There are some difficult or unusual occasions when teachers have to use special care, as when children have witnessed the death of a classmate or teacher. Witnesses will hesitate to return to the scene of the accident. There may be feelings of guilt for those who were directly involved in the situation, as well as for those who weren't. Children, like adults, fantasize that they could have somehow prevented the incident.

Children can be helped to work through their feelings by sharing. Remember to clarify and repeat information so they have a clear, factual understanding of what happened at the time of death. Even more important, young people need to know that there was nothing they could have done to change the outcome. This is especially challenging since we tend to blame accidents on people and things.

Children work through the difficult times in their lives during play. You may even see reenacting of traumatic situations. While such behaviors can seem cruel, don't fear psychological damage. Repetition helps children gain understanding and control of these painful events. Use these opportunities to stimulate group discussion. Ask how your students feel, what they think happened, or even what they wished could have happened.

Preschoolers and primary graders make reenactment into a game, sometimes with hostility or aggression. This doesn't mean they are insensitive; rather, it is an attempt at mastery. Let small children act out their feelings and fantasies. Brief talks afterward in groups or on a one-to-one basis help children express their feelings and perceptions of the event. Ask them directly, "Is this how you think Sandi got hurt and died?" This is an invaluable time for you to clarify any misunderstandings.

When death results from a long or chronic illness the atmosphere in the classroom can be quite tense. Students usually know the seriousness of an illness especially when there are repeated absences and physical changes in the ill child. Class involvement and understanding often depend on the openness of the family.

Sarah's family decided to keep her illness a secret from the school and the community; she was treated in a nearby town for lymphatic cancer. Her absences were hidden with a variety of excuses just as her hair loss was hidden with a wig. Rumors were rampant but neither her classmates nor neighbors ever shared this family's tragedy. Sarah died two years later. At the funeral, Sarah's parents were faced with confused and hurt friends. In fact, the family members themselves were angry that more community members and school friends hadn't come to pay their last respects. The parents learned later that many knew the truth of Sarah's illness but maintained the "conspiracy of silence" established early on. Unfortunately, the family remained isolated . . . even in their grief.

Frequent remissions—when a friend appears to be healthy one week and hospitalized the next—puzzle fellow classmates. When death follows a long illness, children focus on treatment issues: "Why didn't the medicine work?" "Couldn't the doctor make her better?" Answers to these questions are difficult. We have to explain that sometimes medicines are just not enough to help a very sick body. The school nurse will help answer your own questions before you talk to the children. You'll find that children's fears center on the contagiousness of a disease: "Can I get sick from Michael?" Tell children that fatal illness is not like an everyday cold or viral infection. Give truthful reassurance, several times, especially to children in the younger grades. Even when the situations of others are not similar to a child's own experience, associations are still made. Children tend to fear that the same tragedy will befall them.

The sixth graders were fond of their young, energetic teacher. Mrs. Robinson had been diagnosed three years earlier with leukemia. After undergoing treatment three thousand miles away she returned to her class in remission one year later.

Upon completion of a recent examination Mrs. Robinson learned that her illness was no longer in remission and she would have to return to the hospital for treatment. On a Friday afternoon at the end of the day, she told her students she was sick and would not be teaching them anymore. The students in the classroom were speechless. It took weeks for them to feel comfortable with the substitute teacher. Their feelings of anger were mixed with a sense of grief. Only one week before, Christa McAuliffe, another teacher, had died aboard the space shuttle *Challenger*.

It was only natural for these students to think their teacher would also die. They understood the seriousness of leukemia and feared the worst. Small group discussions were especially helpful in this situation. The school nurse also met with some of the children on a one-to-one basis. The students were angry. Mrs. Robinson had not given adequate warning to them. Their anger was also centered on the disease itself. Behavior in the classroom ranged from shortened attention spans and falling grades to general sadness. After five group sessions the children were able to sufficiently work out their feelings and begin to establish a new relationship with the substitute teacher.

In such situations, give children time to talk. Speak with them honestly about the facts and details of the loss of their friend or teacher. "Talking time" and small group discussions do not have to be planned. It is best for group meetings to occur spontaneously in familiar settings, with people children know from their everyday lives in the classroom. Let the topic form itself and allow children to come to their own conclusions. Correct any misinformation and encourage expression of feelings. Once their feelings are identified, children can explore ways to feel better and how to support their friends.

Teachers Need Help, Too

Perhaps the teacher's greatest frustration is not knowing what to do at times of loss and death in the classroom or community. We often feel just as uncomfortable as our children. Faced with the conflict of pursuing academic responsibilities or giving children time to work out their feelings and concerns, the teacher often moves through a grieving situation too quickly. When this happens, children don't have enough time to adjust to the new climate in the classroom or accept unfamiliar feelings. The students themselves can misread the teacher's behavior as unfeeling or uncaring toward the child that has recently died. Often educators will plan only one session to talk about concerns. "After all," they ask, "how many times can you talk about death?" It is never too late to talk to the class about the loss, even if the subject comes up weeks later.

Assess your own ability to lead a discussion with your class. Since the topic of death is filled with sensitive emotional issues, think about your feelings and how you might react while talking to children. In most cases you, the teacher, are really the best person to lead a discussion. If a child becomes upset, reach over to him and give comfort with nonthreatening physical contact—a pat on the shoulder or a gentle touch on the arm. Make a mental note and share your observations with the child's parents. If a child avoids the discussion or becomes disruptive, don't force participation by pointing out his behavior. An open-ended comment is usually more effective: "It's hard for us to talk about these feelings. We get silly or won't pay attention or even fool around because we feel so uncomfortable."

Be Prepared

Reviewing stages of development and children's perceptions of death is the best place to begin your education. Knowing how to help children express their feelings and talk about similar experiences is a special skill. Any of the guidelines given in the earlier chapters of this book will work for teachers as well as for parents. Some modification may be necessary depending on your relationship with the child. Not everyone feels comfortable during these times. You can alleviate your own apprehensions as you learn how children cope and solve problems. Ask your students how they try to make themselves feel better when they are sad or upset. Chances are, those answers will reveal coping patterns. Encourage sharing among your students. They can also learn from the experiences of their classmates. The most useful information you can possess is an understanding of the nature and universality of children's feelings. Griefwork takes time. No one can hurry or shorten the process . . . and it *is* painful.

What Lies Ahead

Several weeks after the death of a student, other behaviors surface in the classroom. Acting out, aggression, decreased attention span, plummeting grades, and overwhelming sadness are among the most common. These are not new problems but symptoms of griefwork. Approach children with sensitivity and caring, a sometimes trying task. While these behaviors may call attention to concrete issues of grades and discipline, the real focal point is the loss. Children are egocentric and feel somewhat responsible for events in their lives. The results can be "out of bounds" behaviors.

Human beings are faced with a sense of helplessness

when someone close dies. It is important for those left behind to feel useful and commemorate the life of the person who has died. Children are no different; in fact, due to their egocentric nature they have a special need to feel helpful. Try to identify meaningful contributions to honor the life of the deceased. Traditional poems, pictures, and letters expressing sympathy are always appreciated by family members. Children have a unique ability to touch family members in many ways. Encourage personalized means of sharing sympathy or memorialization.

Where to Go for Help

Resources for teachers and school administrators cannot be overlooked. Libraries and bookstores have many books on the child's understanding of death. The appendix of this book includes suggestions for children's reading. Books, stories, movies, and even television programs are now beginning to deal openly with the topic of children and death. Keep references in your own library as well as in the school library. Consult with the school nurse, child study team, or school psychologist if you feel the need. In some communities there are self-help groups for children who have experienced a loss; some community mental health centers offer programs for parents and teachers. Remember your own needs during these difficult times. Loss reawakens old feelings in most people. Unresolved losses from the past can affect your ability to help your students in the classroom.

Talk to your colleagues. Mutual support and networking with other teachers and mental health professionals is very important. Surviving a loss is not easy. No one—child, parent, or teacher—should be expected to cope in isolation.

For Members of the Clergy

On many occasions the contributions of a sensitive and caring rabbi, minister, or priest will ease the pain of a grieving family. Words of comfort during a funeral or memorial service will leave a special imprint on family and friends. But finding the appropriate words is not always easy. A family's needs, the nature of the loss, past experiences, involvement in organized religion, and spirituality can influence the clergy's role during the grieving process.

Services

I have rarely heard a family complain about a funeral being too long. When the service is brief or impersonal, family members feel offended that the service did not convey a sense of caring and involvement. A grieving family is not always able to provide all of the details and instructions for funeral or memorial services. Sometimes a relative or friend is appointed to be the liaison between the family and the clergy.

Involve children whenever you can. Don't hesitate to invite them to participate. Younger children obviously cannot have a major role but older, school-age children can read or take part in more formal ways. The chapter on formal mourning practices gives examples of the many ways children can contribute.

The Right Words

Not long ago there was an uproar following the funeral of a young boy killed by a large animal in a nearby zoo. The funeral was attended by friends, classmates, neighbors, and the media. In his eulogy the clergyman essentially told the grief-stricken crowd that the child had been spared an unpleasant life frought with "sin and pain." These were hardly words of comfort. The parents publicly admitted they were shocked and saddened by comments made during the service.

Knowing what approach to use at these sensitive times is a special gift. I would like to tell you about one minister who always seems to have the perfect words.

When Joey accidentally died his parents contacted their church to plan services. A close family friend helped them make some decisions, but when it came time to plan the service the minister met with the family. He went to their home and spent several hours talking to them. He walked through Joey's room, held Joey's baseball glove, and shared memories with Joey's brothers. He looked at pictures, asked about Joey's favorite foods and his school grades. At the funeral the clergyman's words held the congregation of mourners spellbound. He painted a picture of Joey that was real. Every person left the service feeling a little bit better because of his words.

Families respond to personalized, meaningful words. Everyone, no matter what their age, changes the world . . . just a little. It is important for grieving friends and families to recall just how much their loved one influenced the people in their lives. The message conveyed is clear: A person's existence should not have been in vain. If family members and friends can identify parts of their own lives changed by their loved one, griefwork begins with a solid foundation. The clergyman can facilitate this important step by choosing words that are sensitive and reflective. I remember at one funeral a priest consistently referred to the deceased by her formal first name. Since she was not known to anyone as Emily, but rather as Lee, it was obvious he did not know her. Families won't always be able to share critical information. Ask questions, even if the answers seem obvious.

Being There

Clergymen and clergywomen are confronted on a daily basis with those events that most of us experience only several times in our lives. In some cases you will stay involved with a family after the crisis is resolved. Some families want to move on and rely on their own support systems. Knowing who will continue to need you may be clouded by other issues. People are not always up front about their needs. Even when you ask directly you may hear, "No thanks, we'll be okay." Sometimes you have to test the water and learn for yourself if everything really is "okay."

For Others Concerned With Children

There are no rules to determine who can help children in crisis. Anyone can help; a Scout leader, a parent, uncle, or even the custodian at school. We all touch a child's life in a variety of ways. Within your relationship you can reach out when a child experiences a loss. It won't be the same way as a parent or close friend; it will be your way.

Don't wait for someone else to give comfort and support. Chances are, others are thinking the same thing. Children are resilient and very natural when dealing with life's crises. There is a great deal we can learn from them, but first . . . we have to listen.

BIBLIOGRAPHY

Suggested Reading
for Children

The books listed below will help your children work through losses in their lives. I have categorized the books by kind of loss experience and reading level (P–Preschool, PRIM– kindergarten through third grade, E–fourth through sixth grades, and JH–junior high and high school). If there is a book that you believe would be helpful to your children but is too advanced for them to read, you can read it with them. It will be an ideal time for all of you to share your thoughts.

General Information
and Facts about Death

Bernstein, Joanne. *Loss and How to Cope with It*. New York: Clarion, 1981. (JH)

Bernstein, Joanne and Gullo, Stephen. *When People Die*. New York: E.P. Dutton, 1977. (PRIM)

Corley, Elizabeth Adam. *Tell Me About Death: Tell Me About Funerals*. Santa Clara, CA: Grammatical Sciences, 1973. (PRIM)

Pringle, Laurence. *Death is Natural*. New York: Four Winds, 1974. (E)

Rofes, Eric. *The Kid's Book about Death and Dying*. Boston: Little, Brown and Co., 1985. (E)

Death of a Parent

Farley, Carol. *The Garden is Doing Fine.* New York: Atheneum, 1975. (PRIM)

Greenberg, Jan. *A Season In-Between.* New York: Farrar, Straus and Giroux, 1979. (E)

Krementz, Jill. *How It Feels When A Child's Parent Dies.* New York: Alfred A. Knopf, 1981. (E)

Little, Jean. *Mama's Going to Buy You a Mockingbird.* New York: Viking Penguin, 1984. (E)

Mann, Peggy. *There are Two Kinds of Terrible.* New York: Doubleday and Co., 1977. (E)

Schotter, Roni. *A Matter of Time.* New York: Philomel, 1979. (E)

Death of a Brother or Sister

Richter, Elizabeth. *Losing Someone You Love: When a Brother or Sister Dies.* New York: G.P. Putnam's Sons, 1986. (JH)

Vogel, Ilse-Margaret. *My Summer Brother.* New York: Harper and Row Publishers, 1981. (E)

Death of a Grandparent

Aliki. *The Two of Them.* New York: Greenwillow Books, 1979. (E)

Bartoli, Jennifer. *Nonna.* New York: Harvey House, 1975. (PRIM)

Bunting, Eve. *The Happy Funeral.* New York: Harper and Row Publishers, 1982. (PRIM)

Cornish, Sam. *Grandmother's Pictures*. New York: Avon Books, 1978. (E)

Coutant, Helen. *First Snow*. New York: Alfred A. Knopf, 1974. (E)

Donnelly, Elfie. *So Long, Grandpa*. New York: Crown Publishers, 1981. (E)

Hazen, Barbara. *Why Did Grandpa Die?* New York: Golden Books, 1985. (PRE-PRIM)

Jewell, Nancy. *Time for Uncle Joe*. New York: Harper and Row Publishers, 1981. (PRIM)

Jukes, Mavis. *Blackberries in the Dark*. New York: Alfred A. Knopf, 1985. (E)

Orgel, Doris. *The Mulberry Music*. New York: Harper and Row Publishers, 1979. (E)

Townsend, Maryann and Stern, Ronnie. *Pop's Secret*. Reading, MA: Addison–Wesley, 1980. (PRIM)

Death of a Friend or Neighbor

Bunting, Eve. *The Empty Window*. New York: Warne, 1980. (E)

Hellberg, Hans-Eric. *Ben's Lucky Hat*. New York: Crown Publishers, 1982. (PRIM)

Peck, Richard. *Close Enough To Touch*. New York: Delacorte Press, 1981. (E)

Simon, Norma. *We Remember Philip*. Chicago: Albert Whitman and Co., 1979. (PRIM-E)

Smith, Doris Buchanan. *A Taste of Blackberries*. New York: Crowell, 1973. (E)

Stiles, Norman. *I'll Miss You, Mr. Hooper*. New York: Random House/Children's Television Workshop, 1984. (P)

Suicide

Klagsbrun, Francine. *Too Young to Die: Youth and Suicide*. Boston: Houghton Mifflin, 1976. (JH)
Madison, Arnold. *Suicide and Young People*. New York: Clarion, 1978. (JH)

Suicide of a Friend

Arrick, Fran. *Tunnel Vision*. Scarsdale, NY: Bradbury Press, 1980. (E)
Shreve, Susan. *Family Secrets: Five Very Important Stories*. New York: Dell Publishing, 1983. (E)

Suicide of a Parent

Cleaver, Vera and Cleaver, Bill. *Grover*. New York: NAL, 1975. (E)
Clifford, Eth. *The Killer Swan*. Boston: Houghton Mifflin, 1980. (E)

Sudden Death

Angell, Judie. *Ronnie and Rosie*. Scarsdale, NY: Bradbury Press, 1977. (E)
Blume, Judy. *Tiger Eyes*. Scarsdale, NY: Bradbury Press, 1981. (E)
Carris, Joan. *The Revolt of 10–X*. New York: Harcourt Brace Jovanovich, 1980. (E)
Girion, Barbara. *A Tangle of Roots*. New York: Charles Scribner's Sons, 1979. (E)
Talbert, Marc. *Dead Birds Singing*. Boston: Little, Brown and Co., 1985. (JH)

Death of a Pet, Animal

Brown, Margaret. *The Dead Bird*. Reading, MA: Addison-Wesley, 1958.   (PRIM)

Carrick, Carol. *The Accident*. New York: Clarion, 1976.   (PRIM)

Carrick, Carol. *The Foundling*. New York: Clarion, 1977.   (PRIM)

Graeber, Charlotte. *Mustard*. New York: Macmillan Publishing, 1982.   (PRIM)

Miles, Betty. *The Trouble with Thirteen*. New York: Avon Books, 1980.   (E)

Thomas, Jane Resh. *The Comeback Dog*. New York: Clarion, 1981.   (E)

Viorst, Judith. *The Tenth Good Thing About Barney*. New York: Atheneum Publishers, 1971.   (PRIM)

Wilhelm, Hans. *I'll Always Love You*. New York: Crown Publishers, 1985.   (PRIM)

INDEX